I'm Crazy About You John!

To my darling husband to mark the momentous event of buying a home together.

Some of my favorites are: 31, 38, 39, 64, 81, 83, 85, 111, 113, 119, 120, 128, 129, 130, 173, 175, 176, 186, 187, 191, 196, 198 and especially 202 is the truest testament to how much I love you.

Love,

Me

Crazy About You

512 Ways I Know You're the Only One for Me

LORRAINE BODGER

Andrews McMeel Publishing

Kansas City

 For information, write Andrews McMeel Publishing, an Andrews McMeel Universal company, 4520 Main Street, Kansas City, Missouri 64111.

02 03 04 05 06 BID 10 9 8 7 6 5 4 3 2 1

Library of Congress Cataloging-in-Publication Data

Bodger, Lorraine.
Crazy about you : 512 ways I know you're the only one for me/ Lorraine Bodger.
p. cm.
ISBN 0-7407-2683-8
1. Love—Miscellanea. I. Title.

HQ801.B635 2002
306.7—dc21 2002020806

Illustrations by Lorraine Bodger
Book design by Lisa Martin

Introduction

You tumble, you fly, you float on air. You've been hit by a Mack truck, blindsided by the most amazing thing that's ever happened to you. You're wildly, hopelessly, crazily in love, with the emphasis on *crazily*. One minute you were loping along, minding your own business; the next minute your pulse was pounding and you couldn't catch your breath. You've been swept off your feet, and here you are—upside down and completely deranged. People speak to you, you nod, and a minute later you have no idea what was said. You might as well hang a sign around your neck: ABSOLUTELY OUT TO LUNCH.

And oh, my heavens, what bliss it is. What bliss *he* is. He's the only one for you—isn't he? He'll be your heartthrob forever—won't he? You're going to adore him always—aren't you?

Wait a minute. You're nuts about the guy, but there have been others before him. Not to put too fine a point upon it, you *have* had a crush or two in your previous life. So how do you know *this* one is the *real* one? Ah, that's the trick—how do you know he's the only one for you?

Simple: You know he's the only one by the way *you* behave and the way *he* behaves and the way the *two of you* behave. Check it out: Are you filling your fridge with his favorite foods? Shaving your legs every single day? Calling his answering machine just to hear his voice? Is he letting you tuck your freezing cold feet under his warm legs on winter nights? Naming his sailboat after you? Letting you eat from his plate? Are you both inventing private jokes, signals, and songs?

If these or any of the other several hundred possible behaviors described in *Crazy About You* are making their appearance in your lives, pay attention. Listen to your heart: He's the only one for you.

Crazy About You

·1·

When you're around I can't catch my breath, and my pulse does a cha-cha-cha.

·2·

I ignore Call Waiting when I'm talking to you on the phone. What call could be more important than yours?

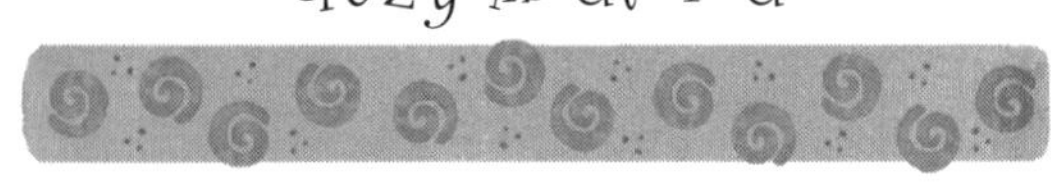

·3·

You bought a
how-to-kiss book and
you practiced on me.

·4·

I bought new underwear.
The lacy kind.

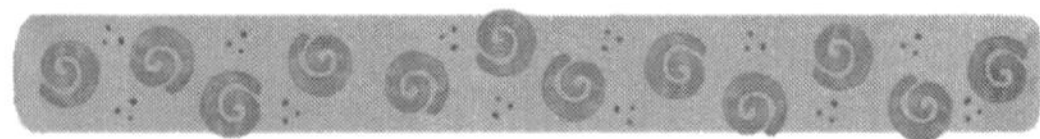

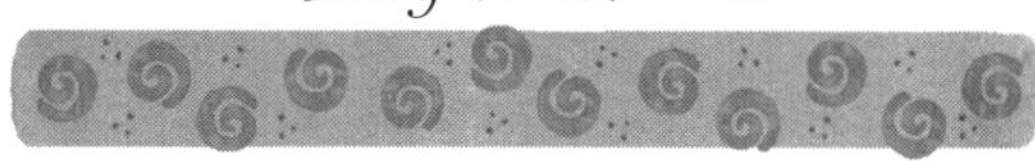

The coffee was ready and
steaming hot this morning when
I staggered into the kitchen.
For this alone I would grovel
at your feet.

·6·

I'd go out without makeup
if you asked me to.
No, forget I said that.

·7·

You may not like your
love handles, but I think
they're adorable.

·8·

I don't mind sharing
a bathroom with you.
(But if you *really* care for me,
you'll find us a house
that has his-and-hers.)

·9·

Your name is my
e-mail password.

·10·

The smell of your skin drives me wild.

·11·

I actually bought you courtside season tickets for your team's games. They cost a small fortune. I don't even like basketball. I must have been crazy. Crazy in love.

·12·

My knees are so weak
I can't climb a flight of stairs.
But, on the other hand,
I feel as if I could leap tall
buildings in a single bound.

·13·

It's a wonder I don't
walk into a wall, because
I can't see straight.

·14·

Sometimes I just sit beside you late at night and watch you sleep.

·15·

I've subscribed to the Romance Book Club.

·16·

I'm going to knit you a sweater.
As soon as I learn to knit.

·17·

In my opinion you're still going
to be incredibly sexy at

a. fifty
b. sixty
c. seventy
d. all of the above

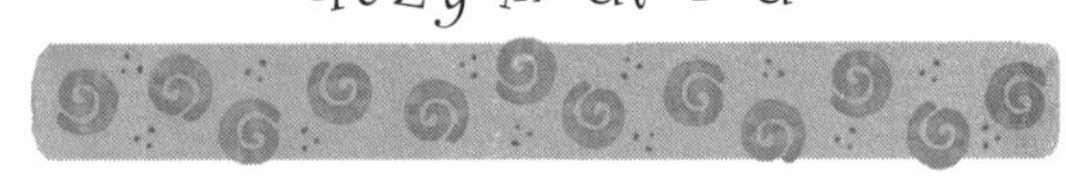

I've always cringed at the idea of going on a cruise, but suddenly the thought of moonlight on the Caribbean seems breathtakingly wonderful—if I can be aboard ship with you.

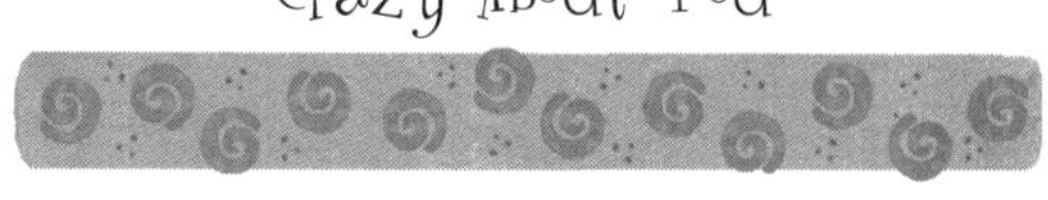

·19·

My mom and dad think of you as part of the family. And you may not believe this, but when my little brother stuck the whoopee cushion under you at Thanksgiving dinner—that meant he thinks of you as family, too.

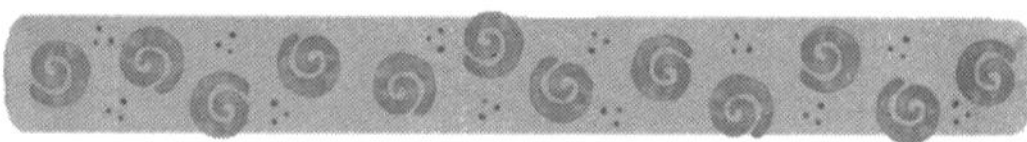

·20·

You program the VCR for me without commenting on the fact that *I just can't do it!*

·21·

You don't make fun of my Barbie collection. Of course, I don't make fun of your beer can collection either.

·22·

I've seen your high school yearbook picture and I still adore you.

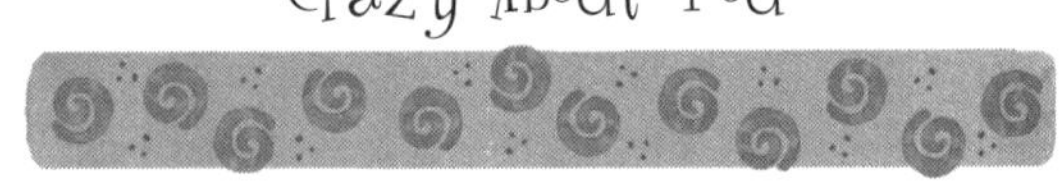

·23·

I know so much about you, I could fill out an application form for you—right down to your Social Security number.

·24·

You threw pebbles at my bedroom window and made me come downstairs to watch the sunrise.

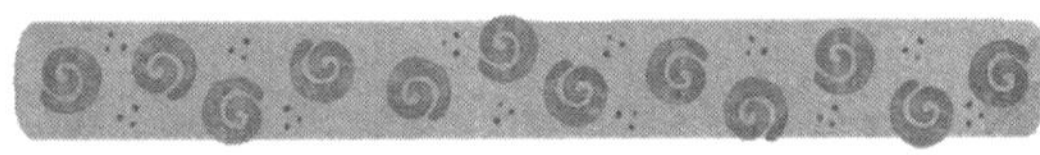

After the baby was born,
you didn't try to make me
feel guilty for wanting to
go back to work.

·26·

After the baby was born,
you didn't try to make me
feel guilty for wanting
to stay home.

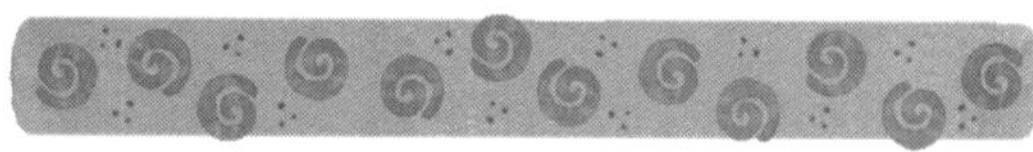

·27·

You were just as excited as I was when we found that treasure at the flea market.

·28·

If I have to hear bad news, I'd rather hear it from you than from anyone else.

·29·

You got rid of your bikini swimsuit, but you insisted I keep mine.

·30·

You searched the Internet until you found a site that sold my favorite childhood storybook, and you bought me a first edition.

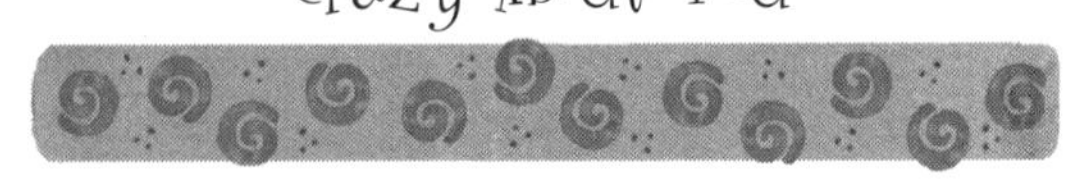

·31·

I don't care a fig
if you can't repair the
leaky faucet, the sticky door,
the squeaky shutter, or the
wobbly table. You fix me up
when I'm falling apart, and
that's enough for me.

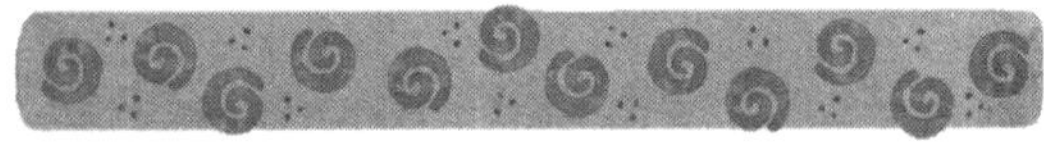

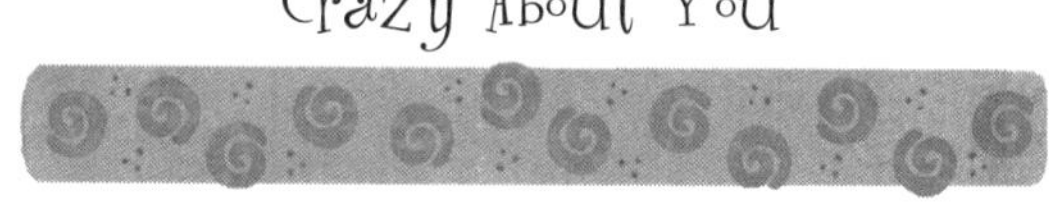

·32·

You gave me a cashmere sweater, and you told me you love to touch me when I'm wearing it. One of these days I'm going to take it off, but not yet.

·33·

Ditching me wasn't part of your midlife crisis.

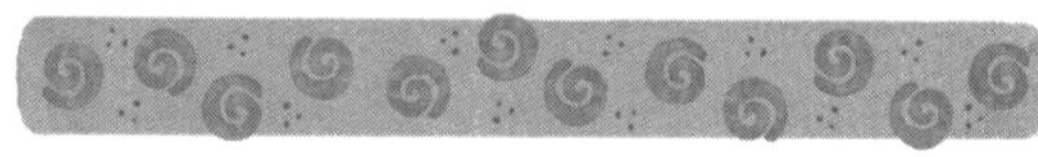

·34·

You named your sailboat after me.

·35·

My previously intelligent and multifaceted conversation has shrunk to one topic: you.

·36·

When I had a craving for pickles at midnight, you got up and went out to get them. And I wasn't even pregnant.

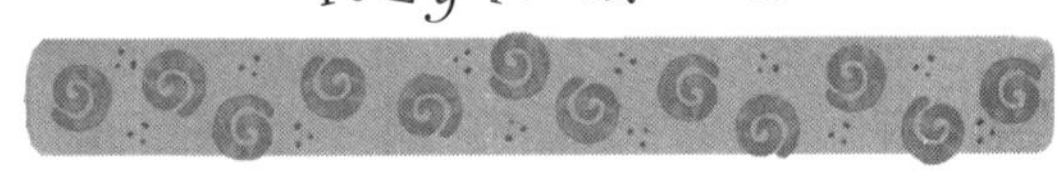

·37·

You have never, ever groaned,
"You sound just like my mom"
even though I *do* sometimes
sound like her.

·38·

You let me eat
from your plate.

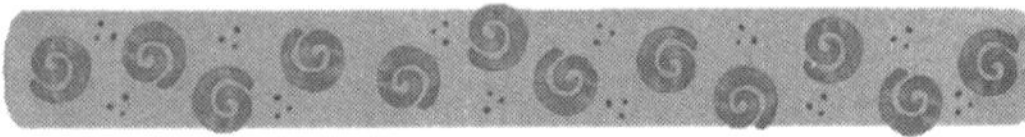

·39·

When I have terrible cramps,
you bring me tea, crackers,
the heating pad, and a
giant bottle of aspirin.

·40·

You let me tuck my freezing
cold feet under your warm legs.
Once. Then you bought me
a pair of wool socks.

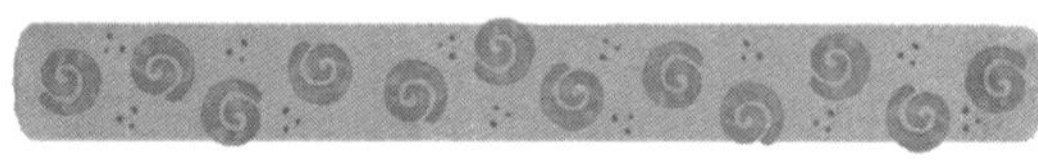

·41·

I'd rather spend New Year's Eve alone with you than go to the fanciest party in town.

·42·

You went to my best friend's baby shower and you actually participated in the games, smiling all the while.

·43·

You made me a tape of
all my favorite love songs—
and another tape of all
our favorite love songs.

·44·

I wouldn't be embarrassed
to ask you for a loan, and
I wouldn't be embarrassed
if you asked me for one.

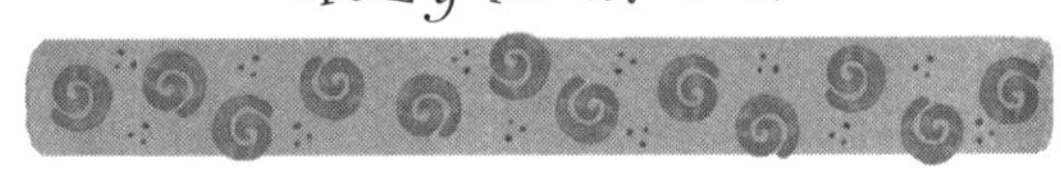

·45·

We bought matching cell phones so we could stay in touch.

·46·

You brought me videos of my favorite movies when I was sick in bed.

·47·

I've started shaving my legs every day.

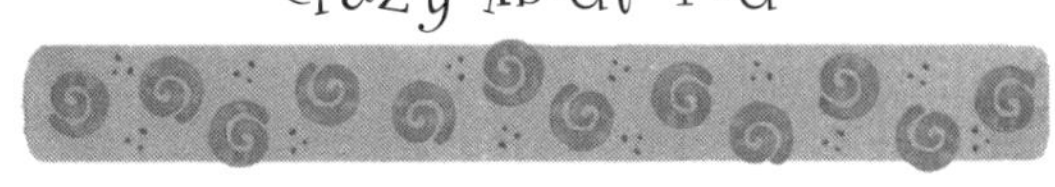

·48·

You've got me so flustered that I'm losing it: first my appointment book, then my glasses, then my keys, then my checkbook.

·49·

You encouraged me to change careers when I was so unhappy at my job.

·50·

If you break a date with me, I know it's only because you absolutely have to. But I'm still disappointed.

·51·

You gave me
• miniature roses
• a Palm Pilot
• a four-leaf clover
• diamond studs for my ears
It's the little things that count.

·52·

Being with you chases away my blues. You're my sunshine.

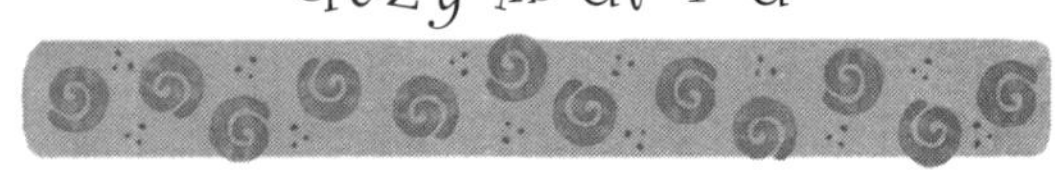

·53·

I get gooey over
your baby pictures.

·54·

Meeting you at the
airport is one of my all-time
biggest thrills.

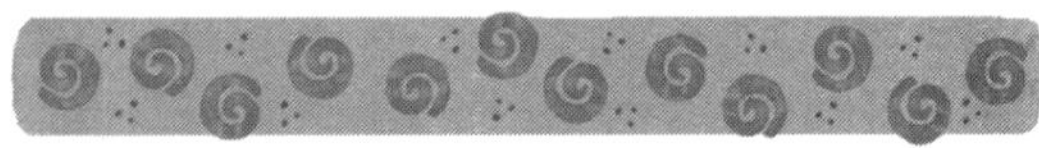

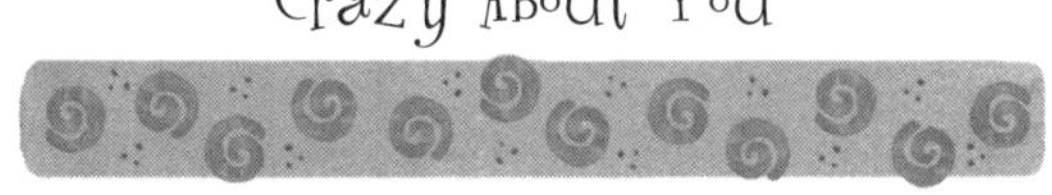

·55·

I'm never a last-minute thought to you.

·56·

When you're tearing your hair out over a crucial deadline, I'll do the laundry *and* the grocery shopping.

·57·

You snuck out and switched the place cards at a formal dinner party so we could sit side by side.

·58·

You took such good care of me when my mom was in the hospital. How can I thank you enough?

·59·

I sent flowers to your secretary to show her that I appreciate how well she takes care of you. (And to remind her of my existence, in case she's eyeing you with too much interest.)

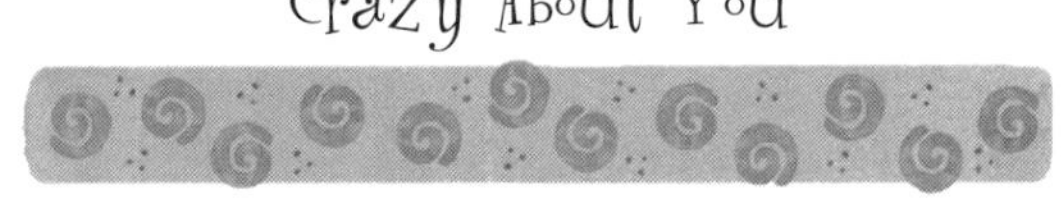

·60·

We were out with friends and you wrote me a love note on a paper napkin and secretly pushed it over to my side of the table.

·61·

You picked a day and declared it our own special annual holiday.

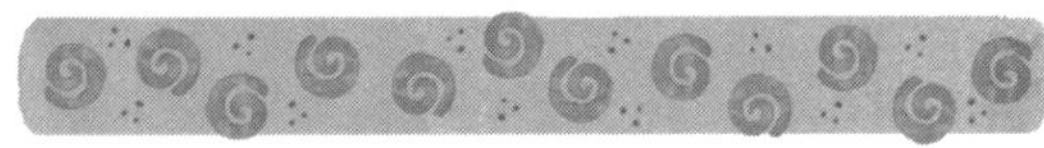

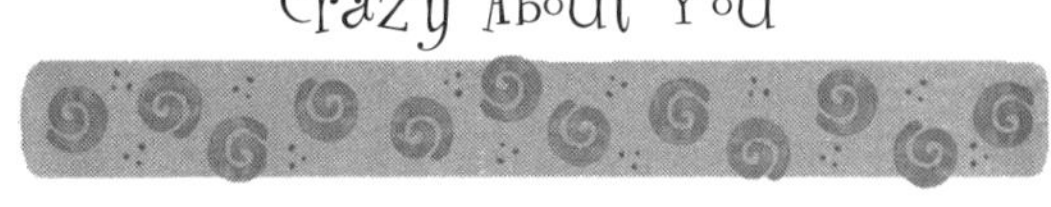

·62·

When I'm sick and scared, you phone the doctor for me. And if she tells you I should come down to the office, you go with me.

·63·

When you whisper in my ear, I lose my mind.

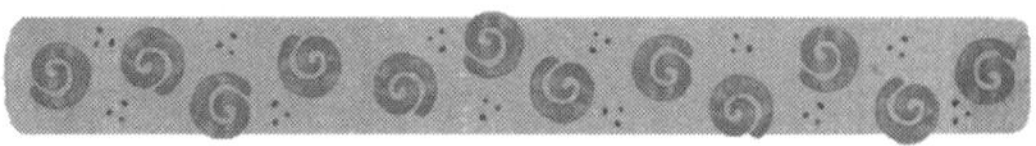

·64·

You sit patiently and make the right noises when I play show-and-tell after a shopping spree.

·65·

You're concerned about me,
but you're not *worried.*
And you understand the
distinction between the two.

·66·

If there's something you
really don't want to do, you let
me know so I don't waste my
breath asking you to do it.

·67·

Garage sales and tag sales are your favorite thing to do on a summer afternoon. Mine, too.

·68·

You never forget my birthday or our anniversary.

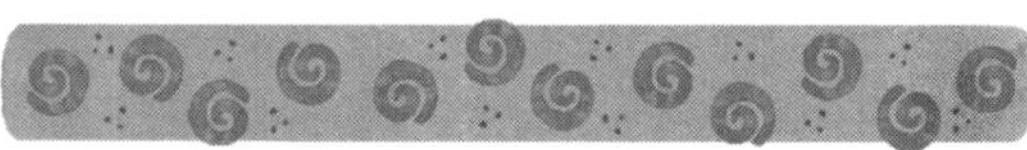

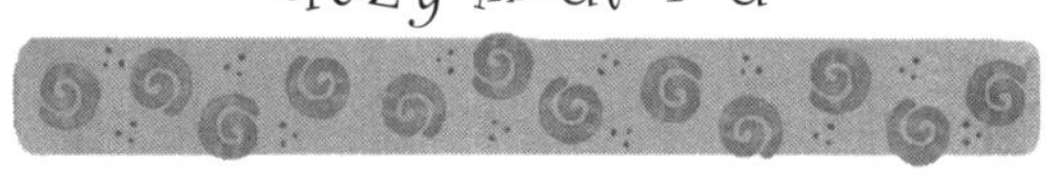

·69·

Cuddling, snuggling,
nestling, nuzzling.
Need I say more?

·70·

You hate my
ex-husband so
I don't have to.

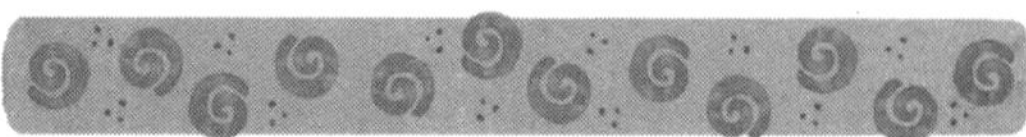

·71·

You don't ogle other women when we're out together.

·72·

When we're planning to meet, I'm on pins and needles until you arrive.

·73·

I can grin and bear it gladly
when you feel the need to
explain in gruesome detail

a. how computers work
b. the intricacies of soccer
c. why you loathe your older brother
d. quarks
e. the plots of the last six films
you've seen

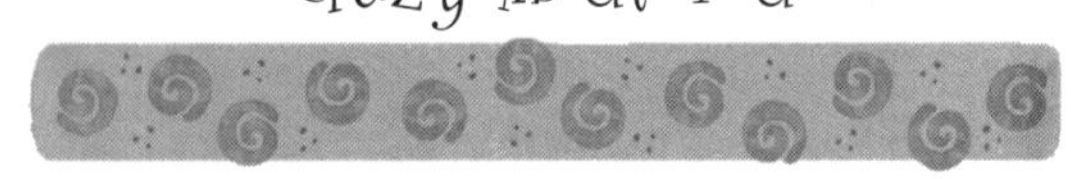

·74·

I let *you* do the Sunday crossword puzzle.

·75·

You have friendships that have lasted for decades. An excellent sign for our future.

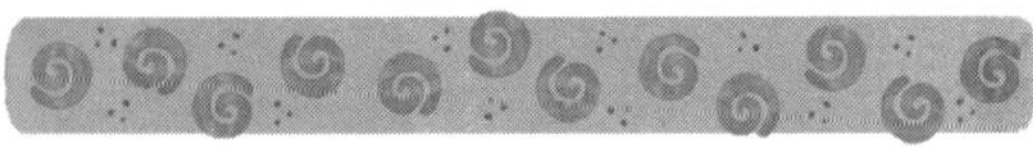

·76·

When the hour for saying good night is near, I start to miss you even though you're still with me.

·77·

I think your morning grumpiness is endearing. But don't keep it up all day.

·78·

The best photo
anyone ever took of me
was taken by—you!

·79·

You never complain
about the number of
mail-order catalogs
that clog our mailbox.

When I got dressed
this morning I was thinking
about you—and I wore two
different knee-highs to work.

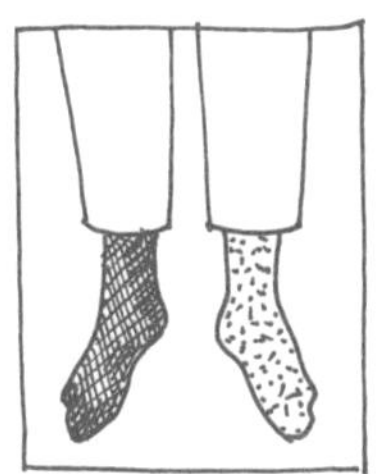

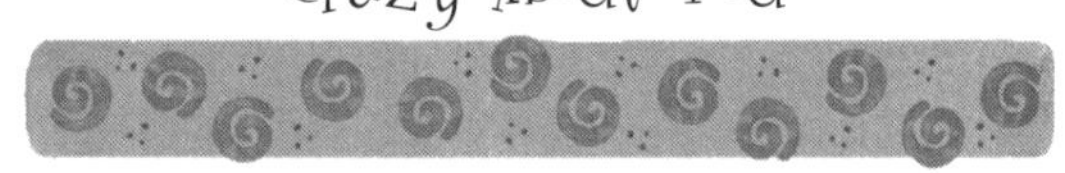

·81·

I saved the ticket stub
from the first film we
ever saw together.

·82·

Doing chores builds character,
and I admire you so much
that I'd never dream
of depriving you of a
character-building opportunity.

·83·

You worship the dog
(cat, bird, hamster, iguana)
as much as I do.

·84·

I count on you and you've
never let me down.

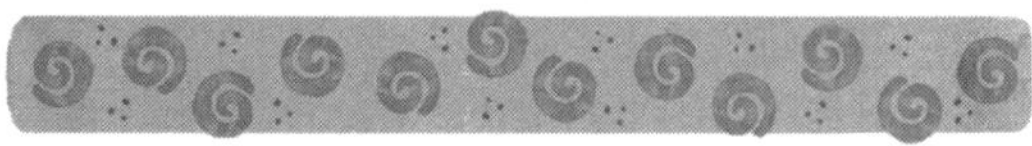

·85·

You're willing to talk out a problem until we've solved it together.

·86·

When you were having your ear pierced, you agreed to skip the ring through your lip. I don't kiss metal.

·87·

I'll discuss, without getting mad,

a. having a baby
b. having another baby
c. moving to a different city for your job
d. letting your parents move in for a month
e. none of the above

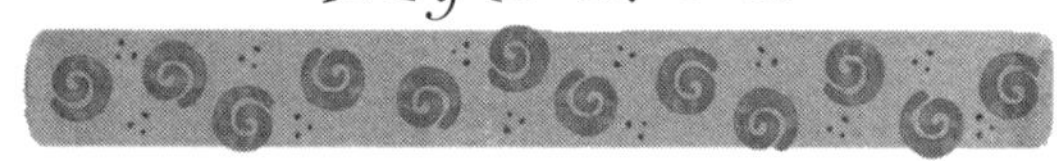

·88·

You happened to find my diary in a bureau drawer—but you didn't read it. Now *that's* what I call a man with self-control.

·89·

You rate an "A" for the Ds: dependability, discretion, decency, devotion, depth. And especially for dash, dazzle, and deliciousness.

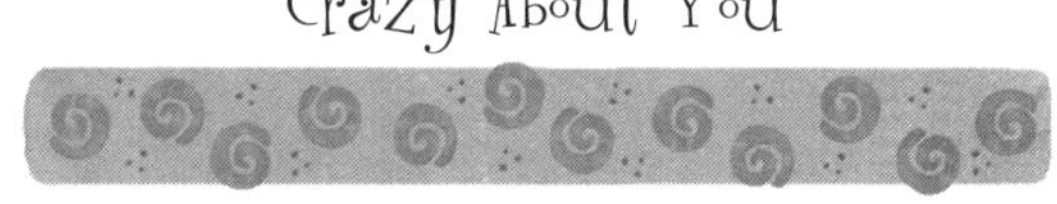

·90·

Fourth of July fireworks
are nothing compared to the
fireworks you set off for me
every day of the year.

·91·

You took tango lessons with me.
And hey—you didn't look the
slightest bit ridiculous doing
dips and turns out on the floor.

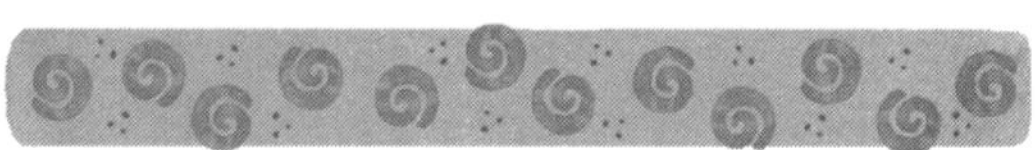

·92·

Holidays with your family are just as much fun as holidays with mine.

·93·

You write a terrific thank-you note.

·94·

You cry at movies and parades.

·95·

Our energy levels match.

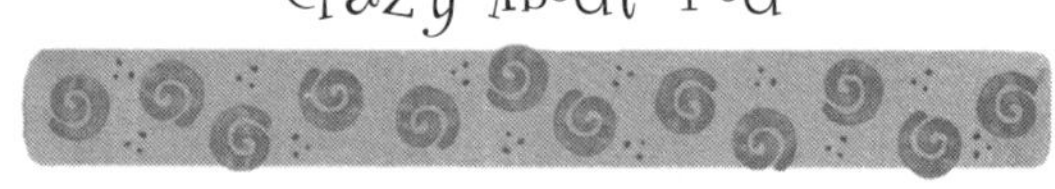

·96·

I'm disappointed—very disappointed—if you can't stay the night, even when I know you have to get home to feed the dog, change your clothes, and meet your new boss for breakfast at seven.

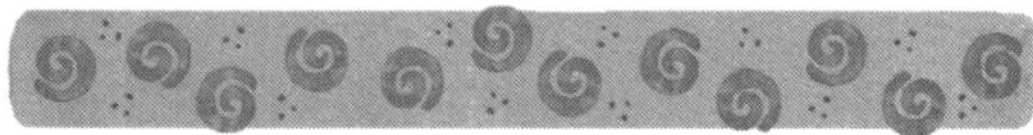

·97·

If I miss my favorite TV show when I'm forced to work late, you tape it for me so I can watch it when I get home. You keep dinner hot for me, too.

·98·

Your life is an open book, except for a few tantalizing secrets it will be my pleasure to worm out of you.

·99·

I don't give a hoot if you're going bald. Bald men are sexy. Really.

· 100 ·

You drove all night
to get home to me.

· 101 ·

You comfort me when
something terrible happens.

· 102 ·

My refrigerator is full
of your favorite foods.

·103·

In spite of the fact that
I'm scared silly of
getting married, I haven't
broken our engagement.

·104·

I telephone you five
times a day, but when
I hear your voice
I can hardly speak.

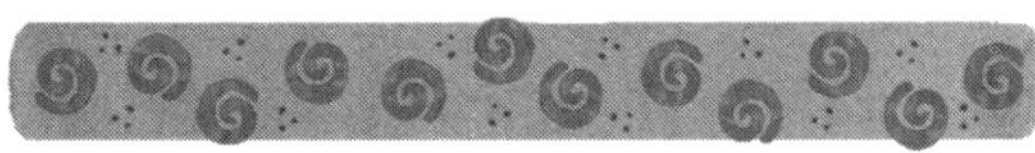

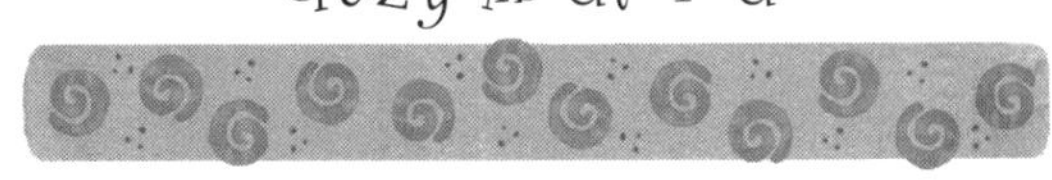

When I lie about my
a. age
b. weight
c. salary
d. availability for social engagements
e. all of the above
you never contradict me.

·106·

Your goals are worthwhile,
and I believe with all my heart
that you'll achieve them.

·107·

When I got a promotion
you had beautiful new business
cards printed for me.

·108·

You never act like the Food Police. Even when I've sworn I have to lose five pounds by tomorrow.

·109·

You never act like the Money Police. Even when I've sworn I'm broke but I come home with a fabulous new leather jacket.

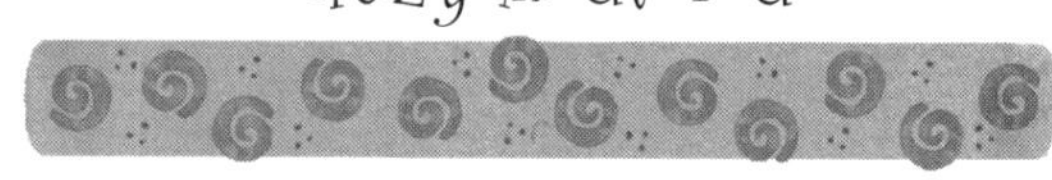

I ripped up all those
photos of your old girlfriend
and you didn't tear me
limb from limb.
(I apologize for doing that.)

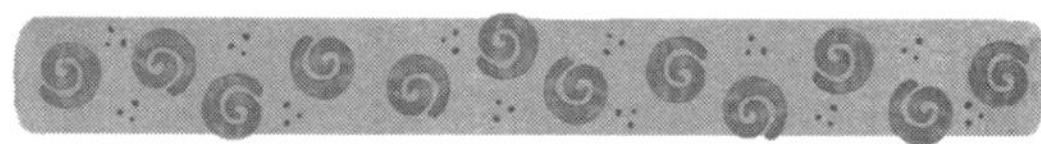

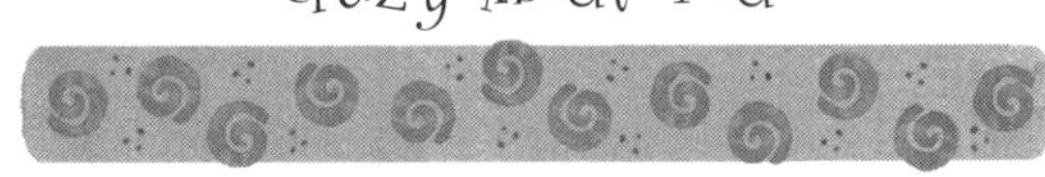

·111·

Waking you at four in the morning when I've had a nightmare is more than okay with you.

·112·

You sometimes call me "darling." That's so romantic.

·113·

You grasp the difference between having sex and making love, and you recognize that sometimes one is fun—and sometimes the other is even better.

·114·

You always give me a call when you're out with the guys, just to hear how I'm doing.

·115·

I would actually try to put more money into my savings account if you asked me to. Remember, I only said I'd try.

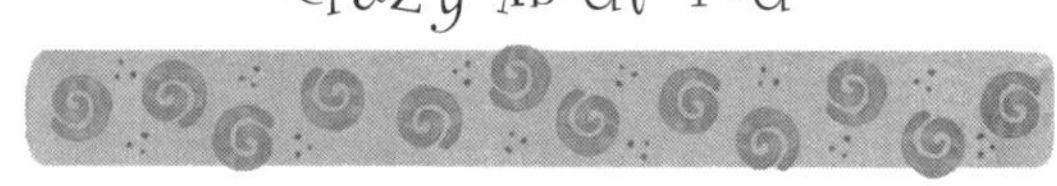

· 116 ·

In spite of your divorce,
you and your ex-wife are
still friends and you're
a super dad to your kids.

· 117 ·

If the movie is scary, you warn
me when the bad moments are
coming—and you put your arm
around me till they're over.

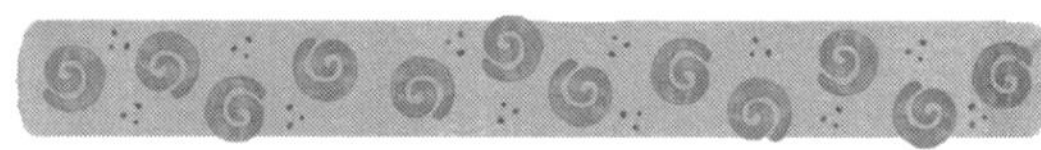

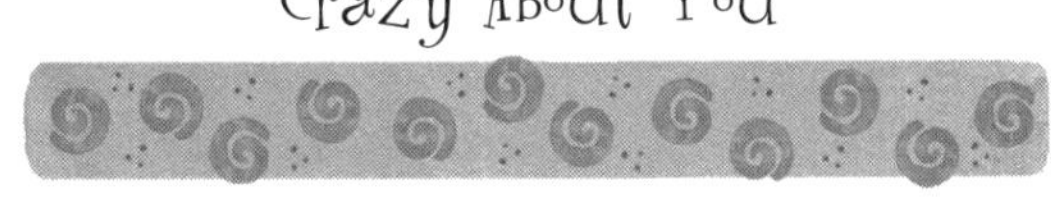

·118·

Your boss came to dinner, and you told everyone in your office that you were blown away by the fabulous meal I cooked.

·119·

You couldn't look bad to me even if you had a runny nose and swollen eyes. Or a bad haircut. Or a hideous case of poison ivy. Not even then.

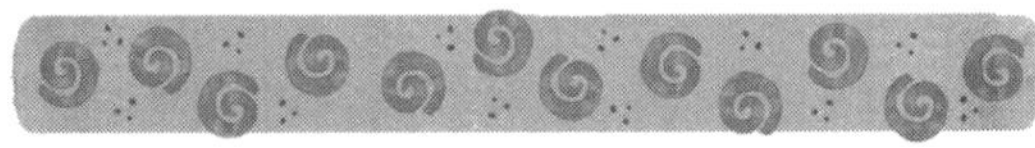

·120·

You warmed the
bed for me on
a freezing cold night.

·121·

I write your name
on my memo pad—
seventy-five times
an hour.

·122·

You didn't ask me to give up my maiden name when we got married, but I did anyway.

·123·

You didn't ask me to give up my maiden name when we got married, so I didn't and you weren't insulted.

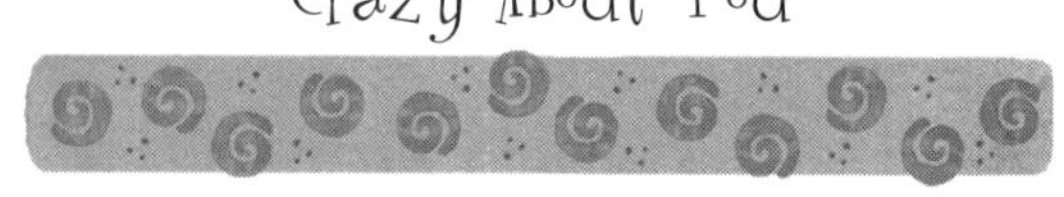

·124·

I've completely forgotten
a. what floor my office is on
b. where I parked my car
c. where I live
d. all of the above

·125·

Slow-dancing with you
is one of my greatest
pleasures in life.

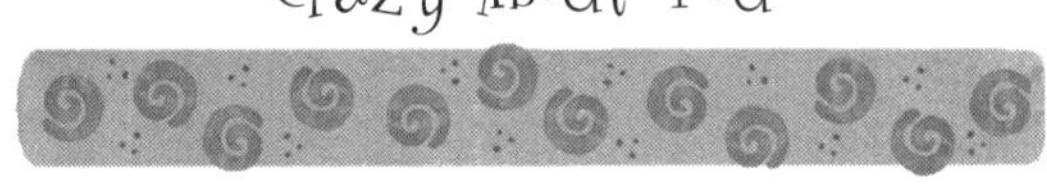

·126·

You promised to add a pearl to my necklace each year we're together. It's going to be a long, long necklace.

·127·

Your support and encouragement have given me new confidence in myself.

·128·

When you put your arms around me, the cares of the world disappear.

·129·

Disappointments are less disappointing when I have you to share them with.

·130·

Joys are more joyous when I have you to share them with.

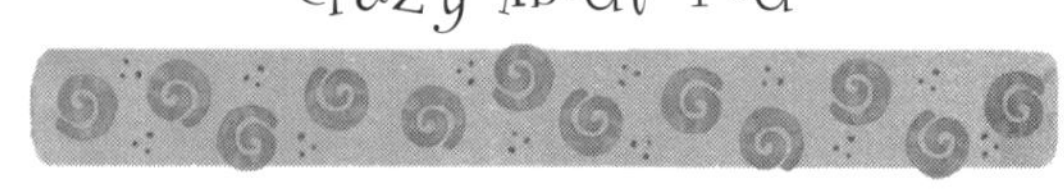

·131·

I'm uninhibited with you and only you.

·132·

Even though you don't like it when I flirt a little with other men at parties, you understand that I have to keep in practice.

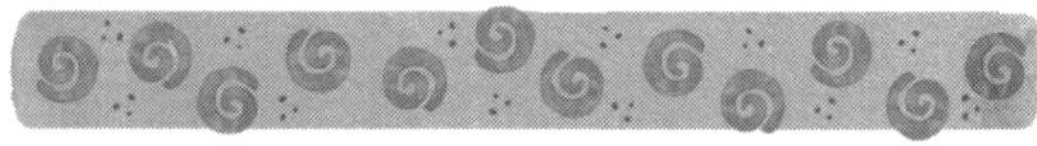

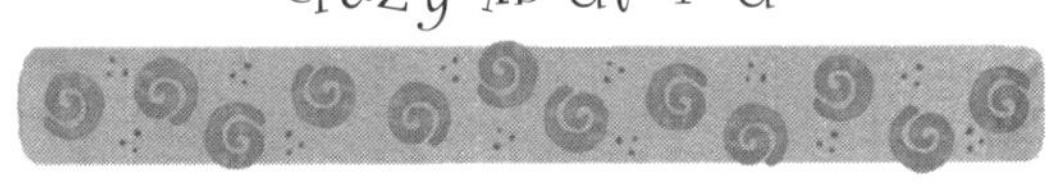

·133·

You bought me a feather bed, and then you convinced me we should test it out right away. Heaven.

·134·

E-mail love letters from you keep popping up on my screen.

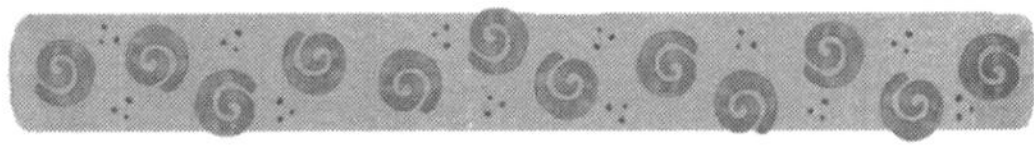

·135·

You never needle
me to sample just one
diet-destroying bite of
chocolate mousse when
I'm trying to lose weight.

·136·

When I think of you,
I spin like a top.

·137·

My scrapbook is full of
mementos of our times together.

·138·

That buzz cut you've been
sporting lately really turns me on.

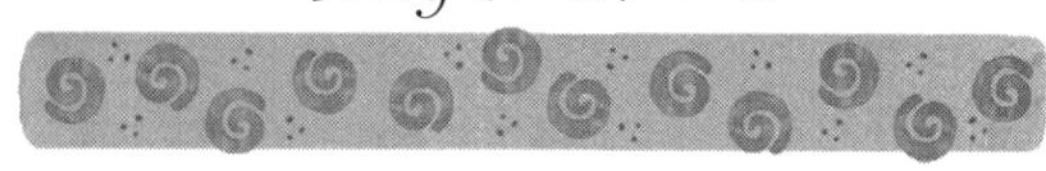

·139·

I keep my mouth shut when you tell me you're having lunch with one of your women friends. Of course I trust you, but I'm not so sure I can say the same about *her.*

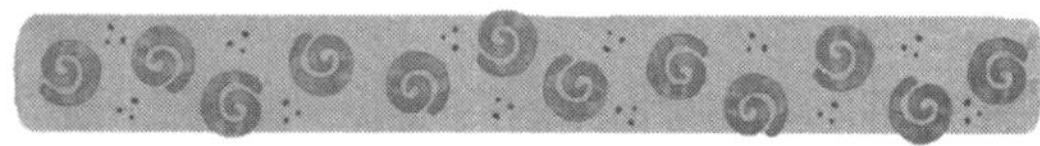

·140·

You stuck with me when I

a. got tipsy at your office party

b. slipped and fell on the way to the podium to give my important speech

c. fainted when I had to have a blood test

d. cried in front of the traffic cop who was giving me a speeding ticket and a lecture

e. failed the bar exam

f. all of the above

·141·

You're the best darned kisser I've ever met.

·142·

I can tell you what the problem is without your taking it personally.

·143·

You asked me to
be the voice on your
answering machine.

·144·

My mom has never been
one to hug the guys
I bring home to dinner—
but she hugs you.

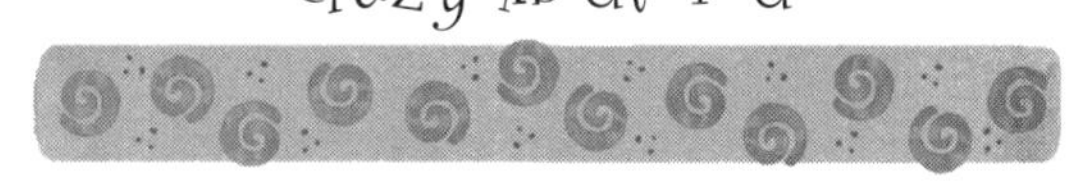

·145·

Saying good-bye to you anywhere at all—even at the front door—is as scrumptious as ice cream because I know I'll be seeing you again soon. The sooner the better.

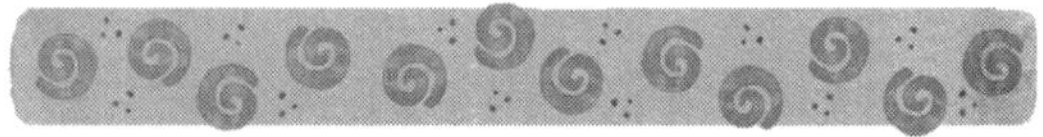

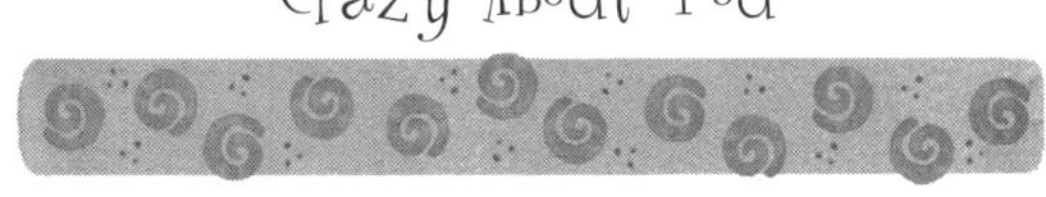

·146·

You hung in there in
the delivery room,
hour after hour after hour.

·147·

You bought life
insurance and named
me the beneficiary.

·148·

I took one of those "How to Tell If You're in Love" quizzes—and scored off the chart.

·149·

I read your horoscope in the paper every day, even before I read mine.

·150·

You're so concerned about
my safety that you insisted I
a. put snow tires on my car
before the first flakes fell
b. carry a whistle to blow
if anyone bothers me
c. install a security system in my house
d. stop wearing such high heels
Hey, three out of four ain't bad.

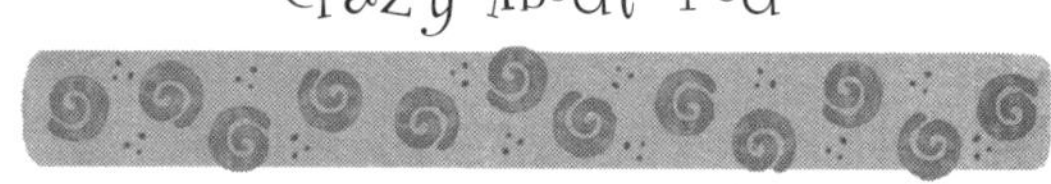

·151·

You load the dishwasher better and faster than I do.

·152·

You pick great videos to bring home when we're having a quiet night in. And you never forget the popcorn.

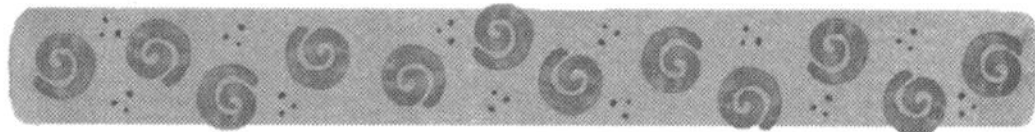

·153·

You actually *like* to go Christmas shopping.

·154·

Going out early to warm up my car on a winter morning is standard operating procedure for you.

·155·

I dozed off during your favorite movie on TV and you didn't nudge me awake. Thanks.

·156·

You helped me memorize my speech, even though that meant going over it seven thousand times. Or maybe eight thousand.

·157·

Every love song I hear sounds like a description of our relationship.

·158·

Special, cherished, and cared for—that's how you make me feel.

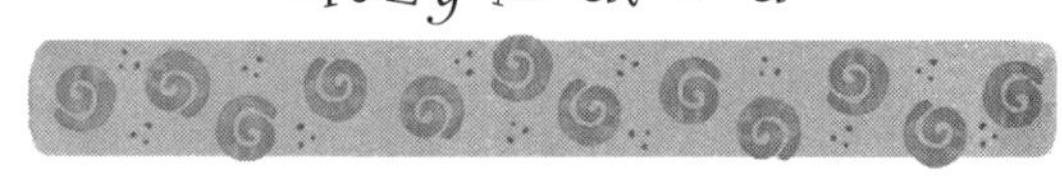

It's totally ridiculous,
but I'm even in love with your
houseplants. Your goldfish.
Your power tools.
There's nothing of yours
that I *don't* love.

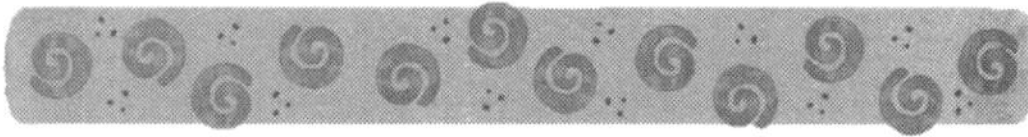

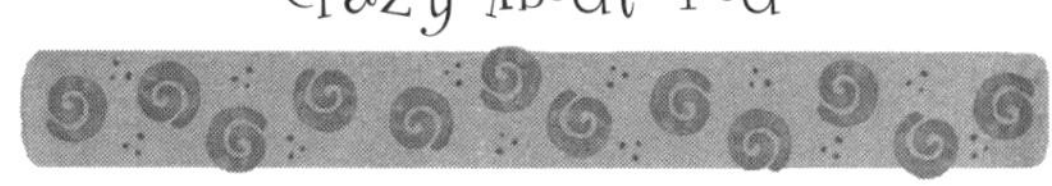

·160·

Making fun of my
a. weird toes
b. stretch marks
c. unusual belly button
d. freckles (not the ones on my nose)
would never even occur to you.

·161·

We can tell each other anything—but we don't. I absolutely do *not* want to know if your sister said I was fat.

·162·

You wore your perfectly nice old tux to the black-tie event so I could wear my completely fabulous new evening gown.

·163·

You clapped like a maniac when I went up to the dais to accept that award.

·164·

You let me choose where we're going on our next vacation.

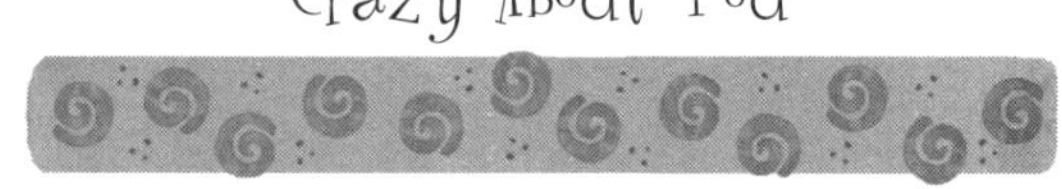

·165·

I want to shower you with gifts, but I know that when I overdo it you feel uncomfortable—so I'll restrain my impulse.

·166·

I cleared half my wardrobe out of the closet so you could have more space. Ouch, that hurt.

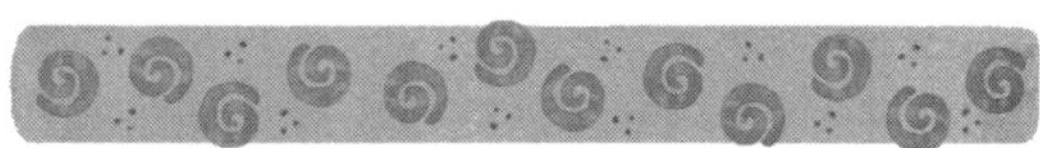

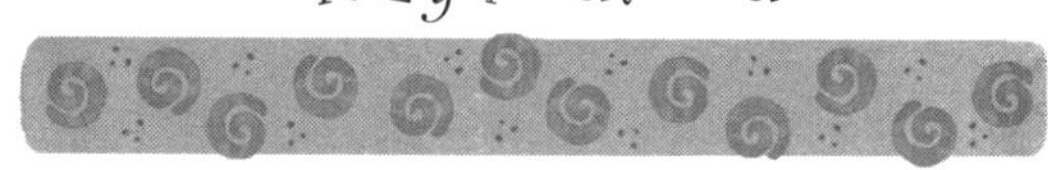

·167·

Your favorite flavor
just happens to be
my favorite flavor.

·168·

Brushing my hair
is your secret vice.

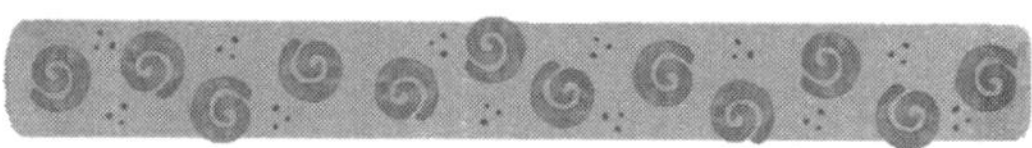

· 169 ·

You agree that furniture shopping must be done together so there are no repercussions when the new armchairs look horrible with the new coffee table and the new coffee table looks only so-so with the new couch.

·170·

I washed and waxed your car for you. (I don't even do that to my own car.)

·171·

When you're out of town I call your answering machine, just to hear your voice.

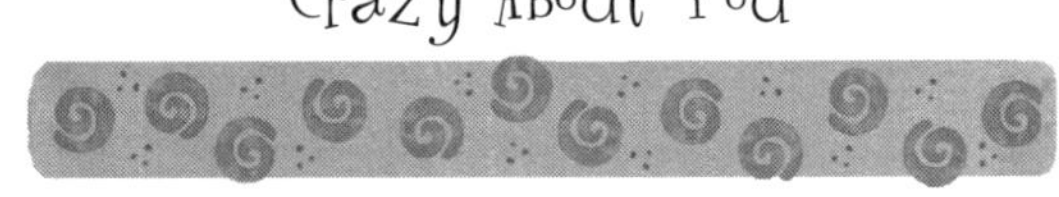

·172·

We're partners, in every sense of the word.

·173·

Sometimes you make me laugh so hard I wet my pants.

·174·

I treasure every gift you give me, even if it's not exactly the one I want.

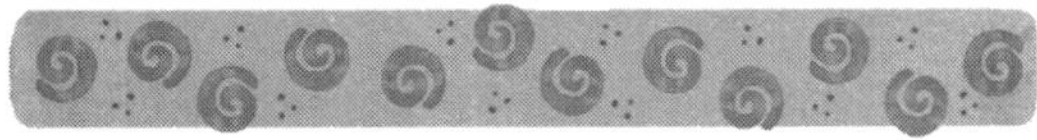

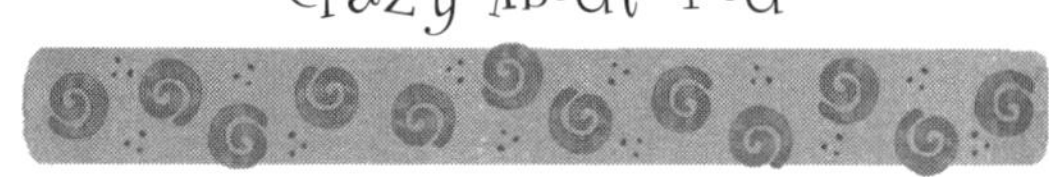

·175·

You offer me the aisle seat when I'm feeling claustrophobic, the front seat when I'm feeling carsick, and the backseat if I'm so tired I've absolutely got to lie down.

·176·

I can trust you not to panic, whatever happens.

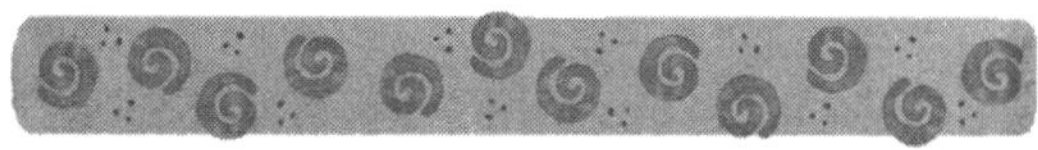

I keep your photo
in a frame on my
a. desk
b. bureau
c. piano
d. dashboard
e. all of the above

·178·

You're not the least
bit like my ex.
Whew, what a relief.

·179·

My nieces and
nephews are nuts
about you.

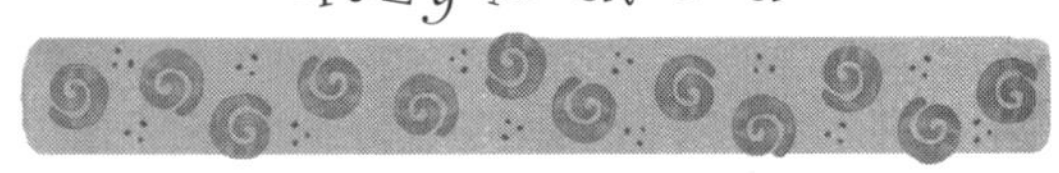

You suggested giving up TV for a week so we could talk, listen to music, read, and simply enjoy each other's company.

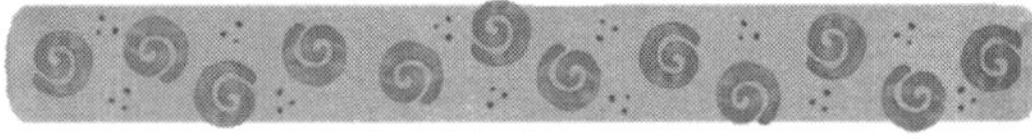

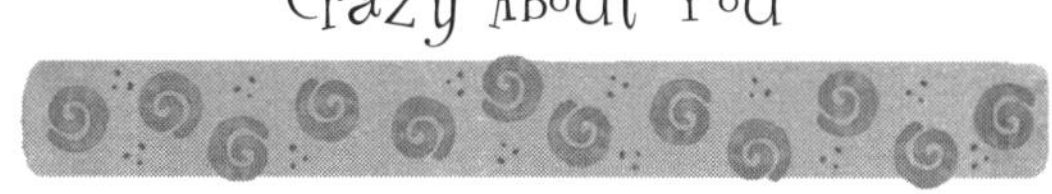

·181·

I'm learning to ice-skate so we can glide over the lake together on a moonlit winter night.

·182·

Marrying you was a dream come true.

·183·

I think we're as perfect a pair as peanut butter and jelly.

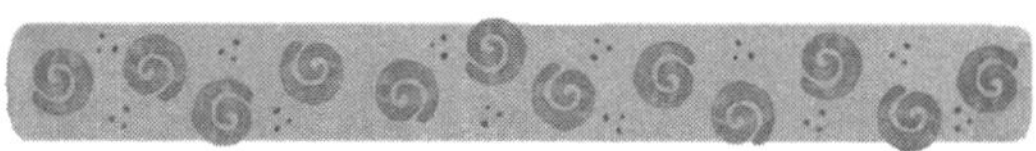

·184·

When *you* want me to succeed,
I'm inspired to work harder
and do better.

·185·

You hired a housekeeper
when you realized we were
so busy keeping house that
we didn't have enough
time for each other.

·186·

You don't mind when I'm aggressive in bed. Mind? It gets you totally lathered up.

·187·

You get a kick out of reminiscing about the good times we've had together.

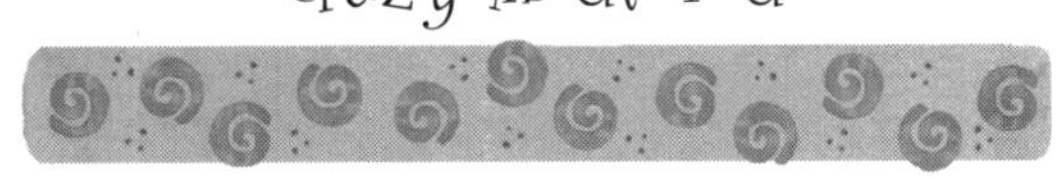

·188·

We share common values.

·189·

You let me use your toothbrush the morning after our first night together—and then you bought a new one for me and put it in your toothbrush holder for all the world to see.

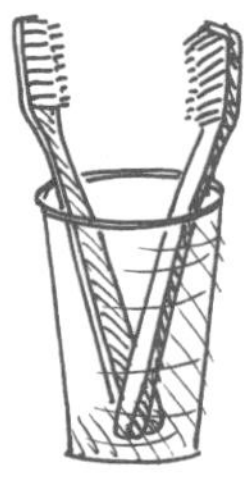

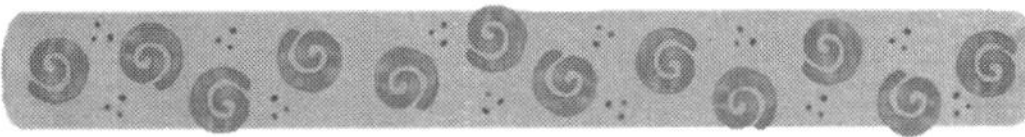

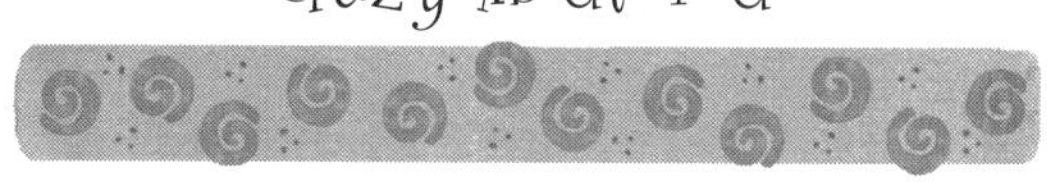

·190·

I'm mad for the nickname you've given me. But I'm not telling what it is.

·191·

You're not embarrassed to go to the lingerie department with me. Now that I think of it, you seem to enjoy it rather a lot.

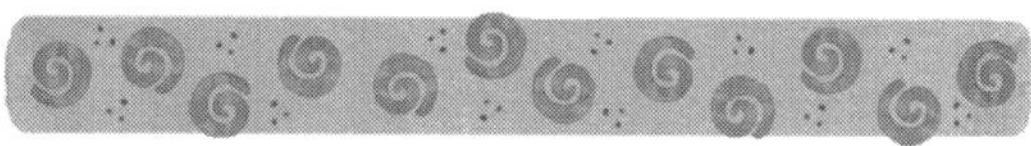

·192·

I'm losing pounds and inches because you've got me too excited to eat.

·193·

Nobody wishes you health, happiness, and success more than I do.

·194·

You know that funny bump on your nose? I think it's cute.

·195·

When we brought the baby home from the hospital, you kept everyone away so I could get some rest. And when I finally woke up you gave me two dozen white roses.

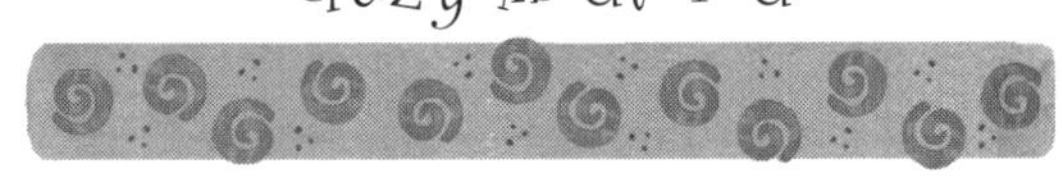

·196·

You're generous.
Or, to put it another way:
You're never stingy with
your French fries,
your CD collection,
your credit cards,
or your Saturdays.
Not to mention your love.

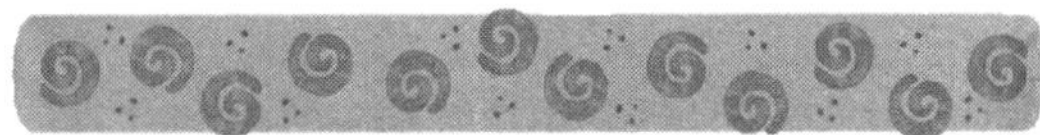

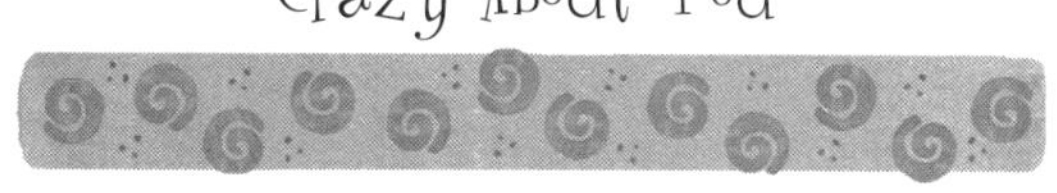

·197·

You're patient.
Or, to put it another way:
You don't get antsy while
I apply foundation, blush,
powder, eyebrow pencil,
eye shadow, eyeliner,
mascara, lipstick,
perfume, and earrings.
Honey, it's all for you.

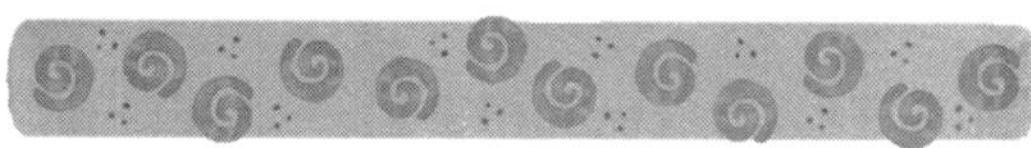

·198·

You're nonjudgmental.
Or, to put it another way:
You don't raise your eyebrows if
I buy a new winter coat when
I already have a perfectly good
one, change careers midstream,
accidentally screw up the
money-market account, or forget
to return my library books on time.
You know I'm only human.

· 199 ·

You keep things in perspective. Or, to put it another way: Couldn't catch the big game? No big deal. Missed the plane? Hey, take the next flight. Dog chewed up your favorite mitt? There's another mitt where that came from. Yeah, right.

·200·

Winter makes me blue,
so you bought me a
full-spectrum light to
make me feel better.

·201·

You're really nice to
my single girlfriends when
they go out with us.
Of course.

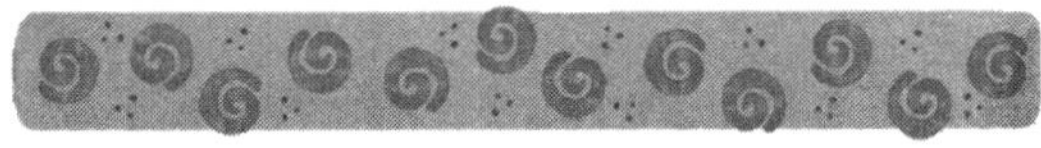

·202·

I listen carefully to your line of reasoning even when I *know* you're wrong.

·203·

I spray my perfume on my love letters to you.

· 204 ·

I'm considering learning to fish. The problem is the worms.

·205·

We went to the playground and played on the swings, the seesaw, the monkey bars, and all that other stuff. How great was *that*?

·206·

You waited for me at the finish line when we ran the marathon, even though it took me an hour longer than you to get there.

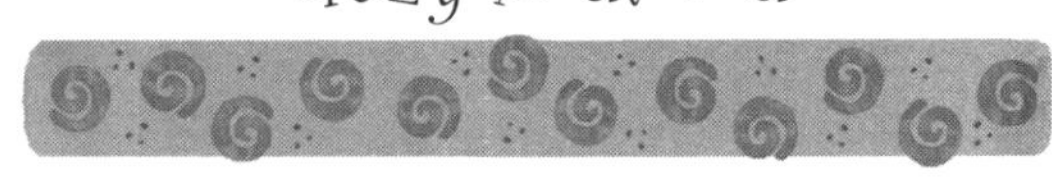

·207·

If I need to be alone for
an evening, you don't
get bent out of shape.
You can be on your own
for twelve hours without
making me feel guilty.

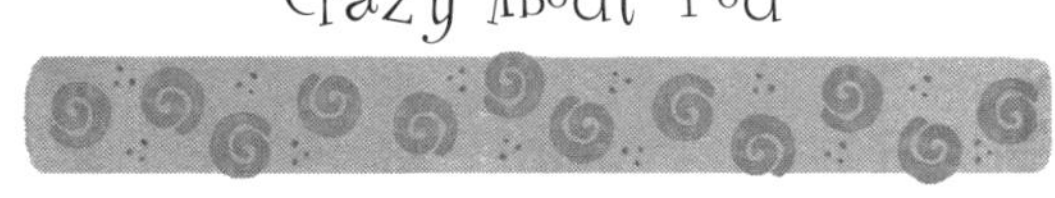

·208·

Locking the bedroom door and dressing up—at *your* request—like a

a. French maid

b. motorcycle chick

c. belly dancer

d. high-school cheerleader

doesn't offend me in the least. *Au contraire,* the possibilities seem . . . intriguing.

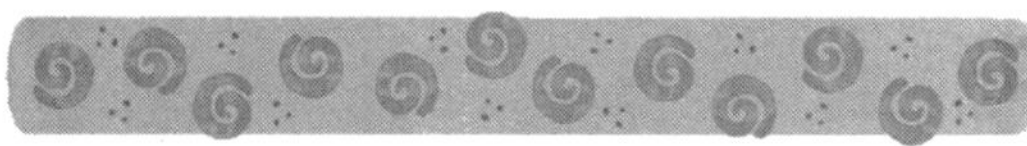

·209·

When I take a bath you like to sit on the edge of the tub and chat. That is *so* cozy.

·210·

You looked at every single one of my travel photos, without getting bored. Or if you *were* bored, you didn't let on.

·211·

You clip grocery coupons and you actually use them.

·212·

You stood on line for hours to get tickets to my favorite singer's concert.

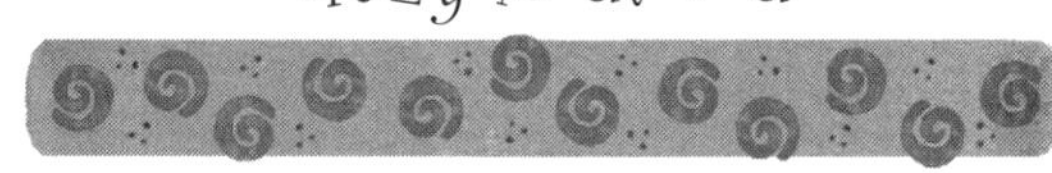

·213·

I can trust you to water the plants, pick up my mail, and feed the cat when I have to go out of town on a business trip.

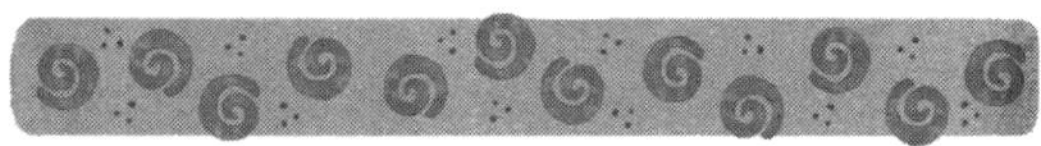

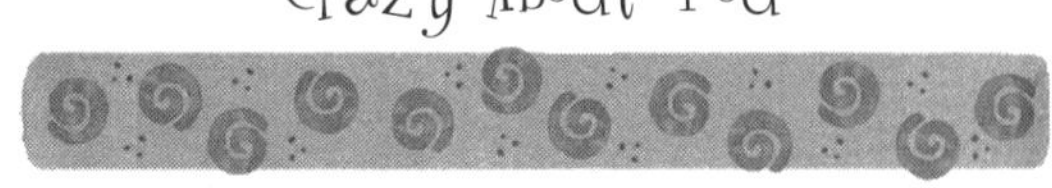

·214·

I cherish beginning and ending my day with you.

·215·

You're my best friend.

·216·

I'd give you my last potato chip.

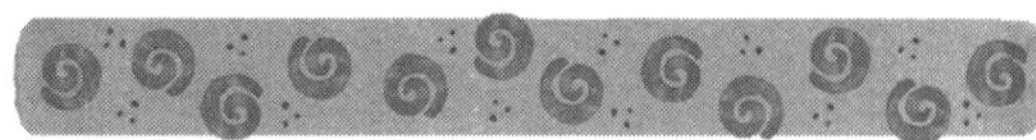

·217·

I'd rather have you
than a dozen
chocolate chip cookies.

·218·

Your mother gave me a truly
wonderful birthday present.

·219·

We fall asleep holding hands.

·220·

Breakfast in bed with you is one of my favorite activities.

·221·

I'd give up silver toenail polish for you. I was ready for a change anyway . . .

·222·

When I'm with you I feel twenty years younger. Okay, ten, but who's counting?

·223·

We have matching wrinkles and gray hair.

·224·

Even after all this time I still get a thrill over you.

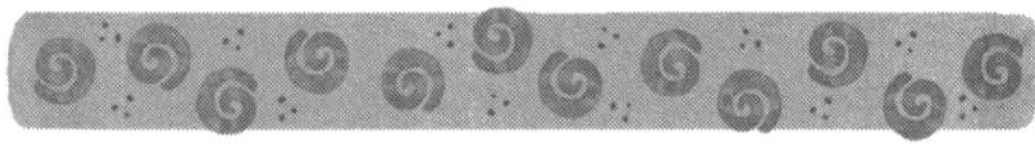

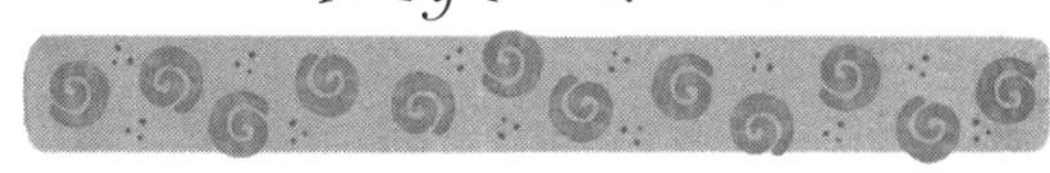

·225·

I'll never ask you to give up your

a. pale blue polyester pants

b. "My parents went to Miami Beach and all I got was this lousy T-shirt" T-shirt

c. white patent-leather loafers

d. beret

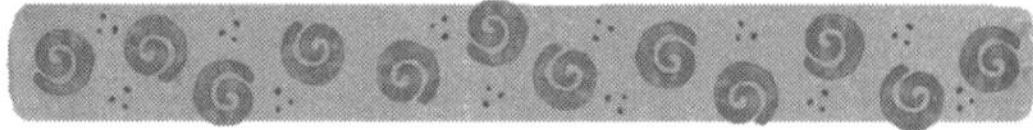

·226·

You have a great handshake. I noticed it the first time we met.

·227·

You never tell me to calm down when I get angry. That would be patronizing, and you never patronize me.

·228·

I overheard you talking to your best friend on the telephone: "She's smart and major talented and classy as hell. And she's so damned sexy." Did you know I was eavesdropping?

·229·

You kidnapped me for a romantic weekend at a charming little inn in the country.

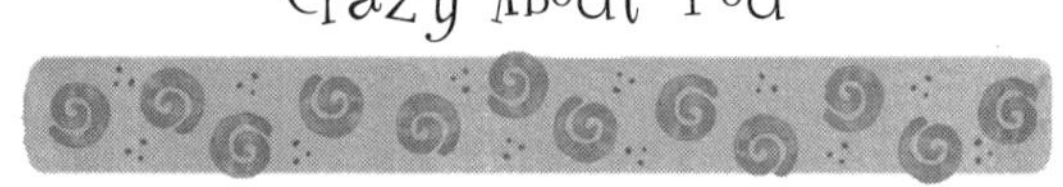

·230·

You remembered to bring bug repellent and toilet paper when we went camping.

·231·

Sleeping like spoons
is at the top of your
Most Favorite list.
Mine, too.

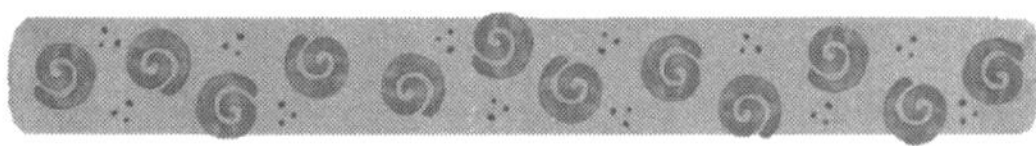

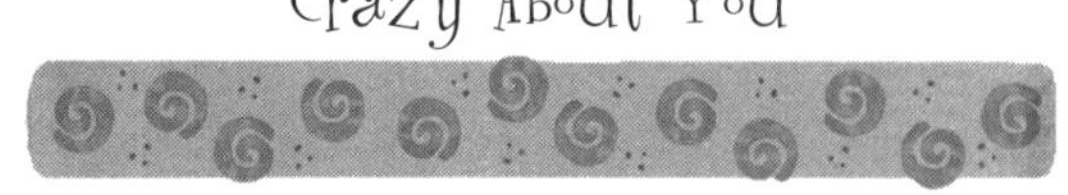

·232·

Being tickled renders me helpless, so you tickle me and have your way with me.

·233·

You're a romantic at heart: In your closet I discovered an old shoebox filled with all the love letters I've ever written to you.

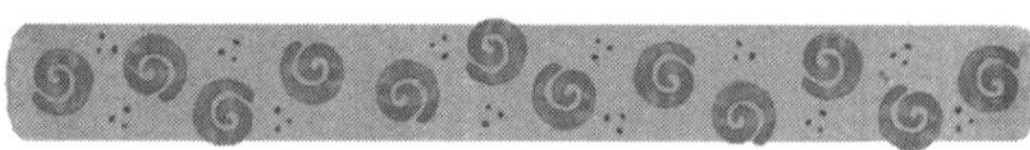

·234·

You bought me a set of free weights because you like strong women.

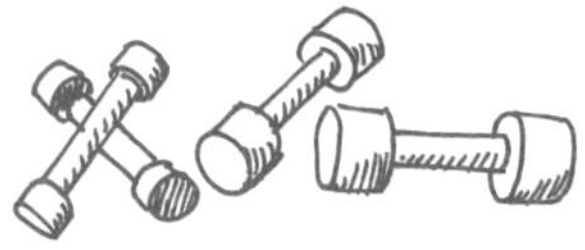

·235·

You helped me plan my get-a-raise strategy because you believe in equal pay for equal work.

·236·

You let me drive because you know that women drivers are as good as men.

·237·

I melt when you massage my feet. In fact, I melt if you even *offer* to massage my feet.

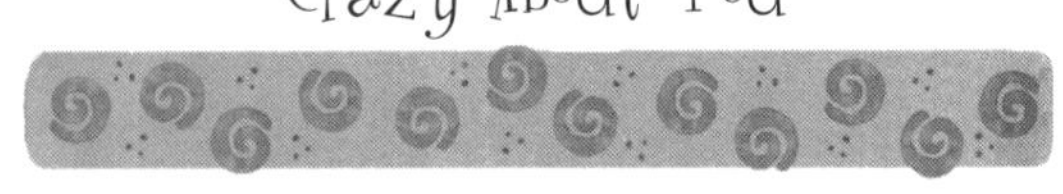

·238·

I'd let my hair grow
if you wanted me to.
Maybe.

·239·

When we got engaged you
put all your bank accounts
in our joint names. I guess
you really *do* trust me.

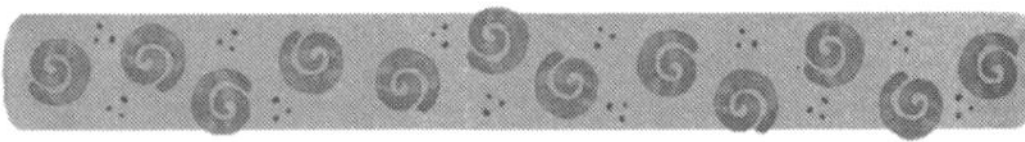

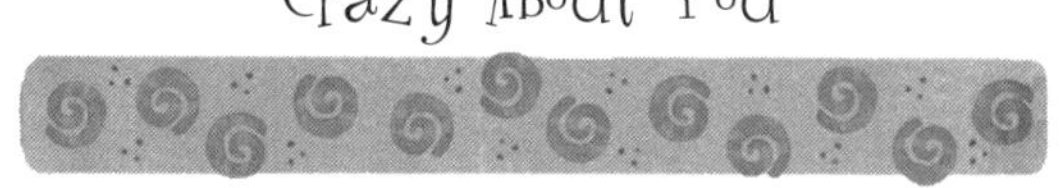

·240·

I wish everyone could be as head over heels as we are.

·241·

I have infinite patience for you.

·242·

Making you feel good makes me feel good.

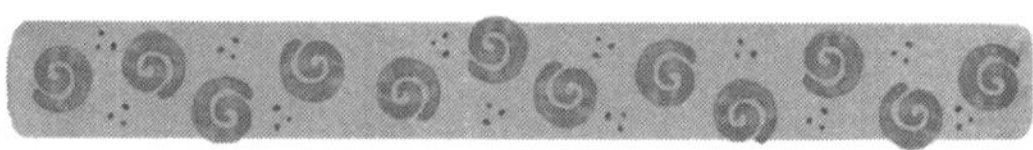

·243·

You rush to my rescue when
there's a mouse, a spider,
a water bug, a wasp,
or a bat threatening my
home and my sanity.

·244·

I balanced your checkbook for you when you were in a hopeless muddle.

·245·

You were there, holding my hand, when I came out of the anesthesia.

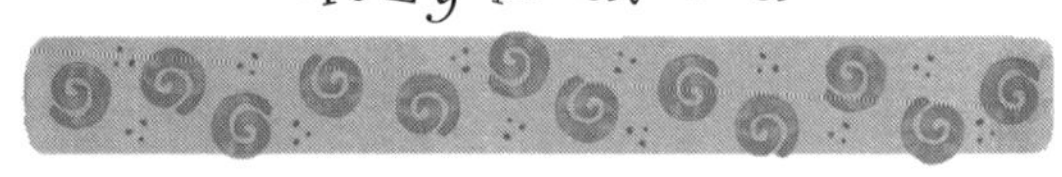

·246·

When we're
a. walking
b. swimming
c. skiing
d. bicycling
you go at my pace so
we can be together.

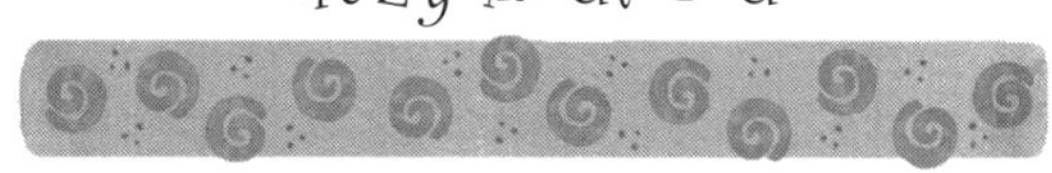

·247·

You cried with me when my beloved cat died.

·248·

I blush when I think of you.

·249·

You practiced safe sex before you met me.

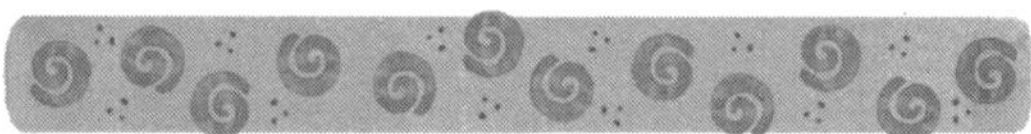

·250·

A huge bouquet of tulips arrived from you minutes before I had to give my make-or-break presentation at the staff meeting. (I went in there and knocked their socks off.)

·251·

You plucked out my first few gray hairs for me and told me that gray hairs are no big whoop. (I made an appointment with a colorist anyway.)

·252·

Sometimes we meet and find we're wearing his-and-hers versions of the same outfit.

·253·

I order pizzas with all your favorite toppings, and you order them with mine.

·254·

You loathe chain letters as much as I do.

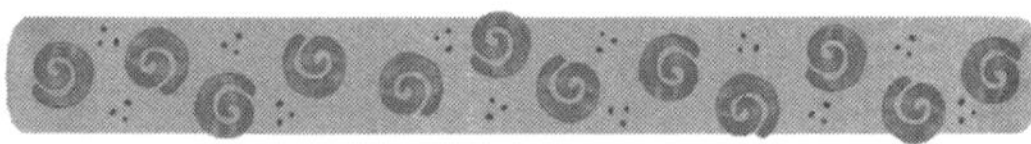

·255·

You like gossip
as much as I do.

·256·

You're disgusted by men
who sabotage their wives'
careers because they can't
hack having less money,
power, or success.

·257·

I'm thrilled when you show off for me (but only for me). So flex those abs, slam that dunk, work that macarena—I adore it all.

·258·

You're not afraid of the future. Especially the future with me.

·259·

I lied for you when your

a. mother

b. boss

c. ex-wife

was looking for you.

That's a one-time favor, babe.

·260·

I'm proud of you.

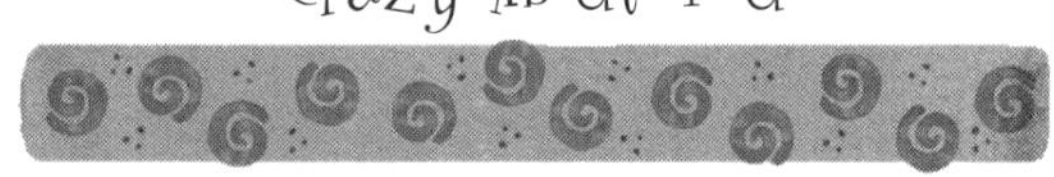

·261·

One smile from you and
I feel like a million bucks.
Two million bucks.

·262·

Your hugs and kisses
are better than food.

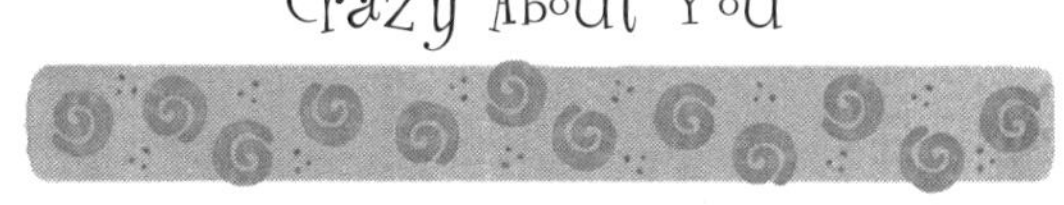

·263·

I've started having fantasies about the way our children might look.

·264·

We get really silly together—like that bubble-gum bubble-blowing contest we had. (I still think my bubble was bigger than yours.)

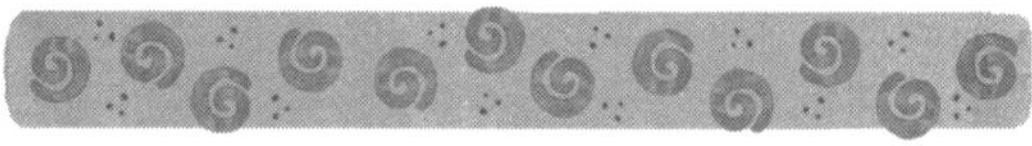

·265·

I threw away all my old love letters from other guys. Well, I didn't exactly throw them away, but I put them in a place where you'll never find them. That's sort of the same thing, isn't it?

·266·

Sneaking up behind you
to hug you around the
waist tickles me pink.

·267·

When your buddy made a pass
at me you wanted to deck him,
but you didn't because you
know I can't stand violence.

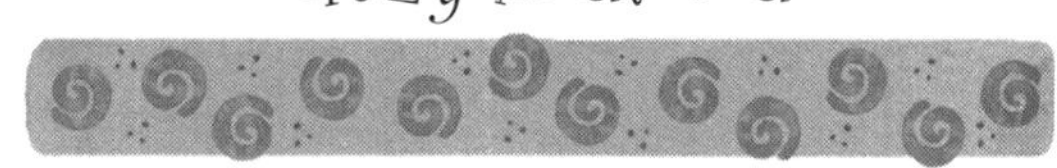

·268·

When *I* thought we were having problems and *you* didn't, you still agreed to discuss my issues with an open mind.

·269·

The plans we make together are the most important things in my life.

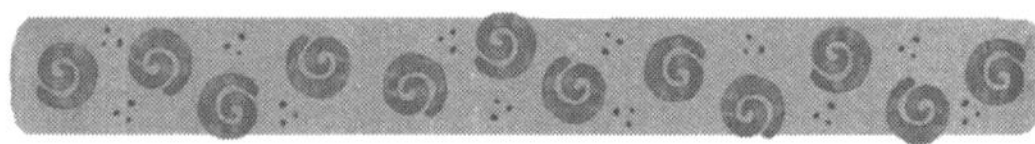

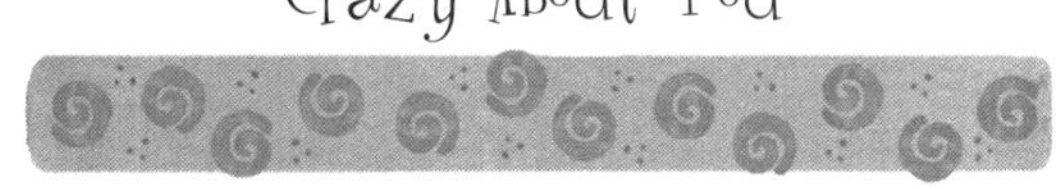

·270·

You like it when I tell you what I enjoy in bed.

·271·

You treat me with respect.

·272·

You're never too busy for me. But if you need a little time to retire to your cave to cool out, that's okay, too.

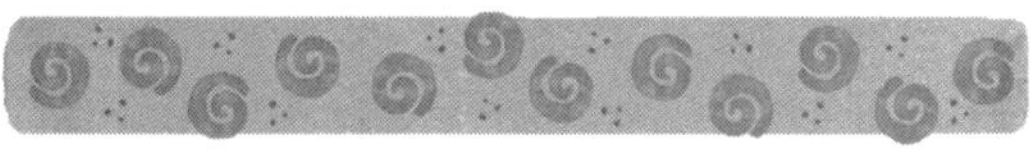

You give me a heads-up if
a. my hem is hanging
b. there's something disgusting stuck to my shoe
c. my collar is poking up in a weird way
d. mascara is smudged under my eyes
e. the tail of my long scarf is charged with static and clinging to an embarrassing place
because you *know* how important these things are to me.

·274·

You humor me: You dash back to the house to check that the oven is off, the answering machine is on, and the windows are closed.

·275·

I find your disorganized closets and bureau drawers charming, not messy.

·276·

I called your mother to thank her for bringing you into the world.

·277·

I bought you a cookie jar and I keep it filled with your favorites.

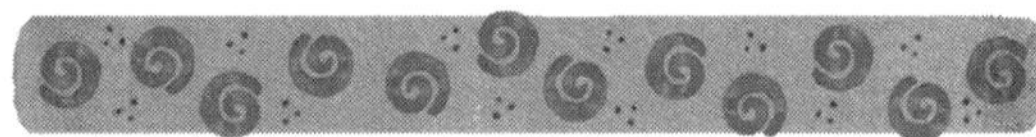

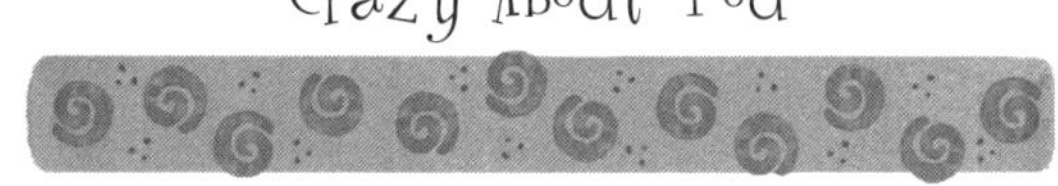

·278·

The way you sing in choir inspires me and fills me with hope.

·279·

You didn't mind when I threw up in your car.

·280·

You let me use your computer when mine was being repaired.

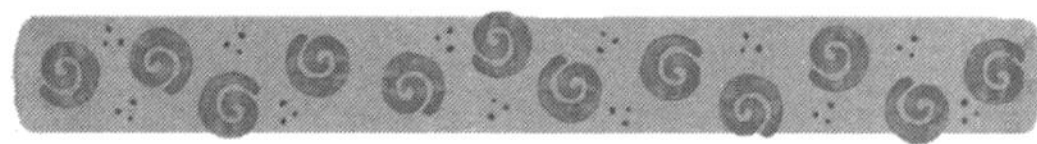

·281·

Apologizing to you isn't as hard as I thought it would be. Just don't expect me to do it too often.

·282·

I'm enchanted by that nervous look you get on your face when another woman flirts with you. Relax—I know *she* went after *you* and not vice versa.

·283·

You told your boss you couldn't put in any more overtime because you need your weekends for your family. Now *that* took courage.

·284·

When the horse threw me, you picked me up and helped me get back in the saddle.

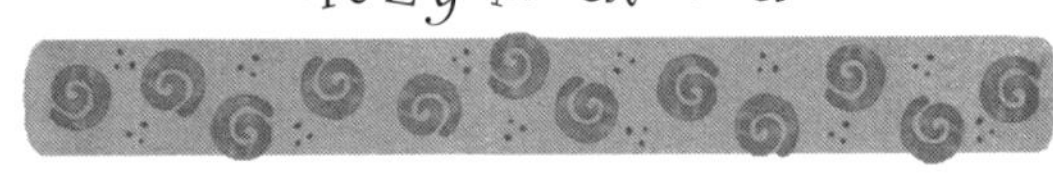

·285·

You let me wear your letter sweater in high school.

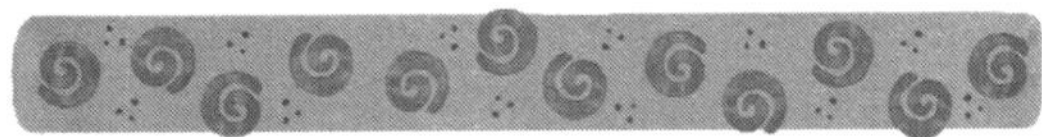

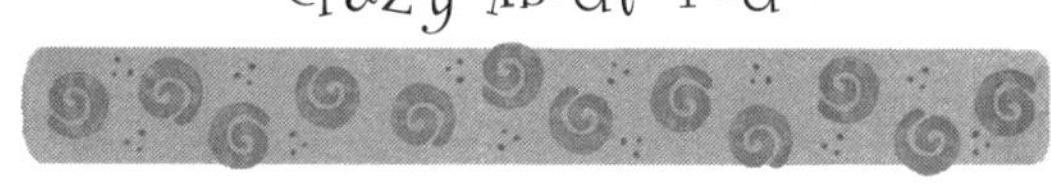

·286·

When we disagree about

a. money

b. the new curtains

c. which car gets better mileage

d. where to go on our vacation

e. red clam sauce or white

you don't throw a temper tantrum

and insist on having everything

your own way.

·287·

You waltzed me around the kitchen until we were dizzy.

·288·

You kissed me under the mistletoe.

·289·

I've heard your stories a dozen times and I'm still not tired of them. A dozen more times— I won't guarantee anything.

·290·

On job applications and questionnaires, you wrote my name on the *next of kin* line even before we were married.

·291·

Though it's hard for you to tell me what's on your mind, you make the effort.

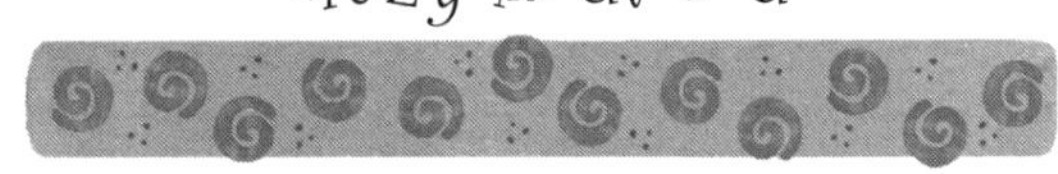

·292·

I bought you a beautiful rocking chair so you could rock me on your lap.

·293·

We can argue about ideas, with no hard feelings later.

·294·

Forgive and forget is one of your guiding principles.

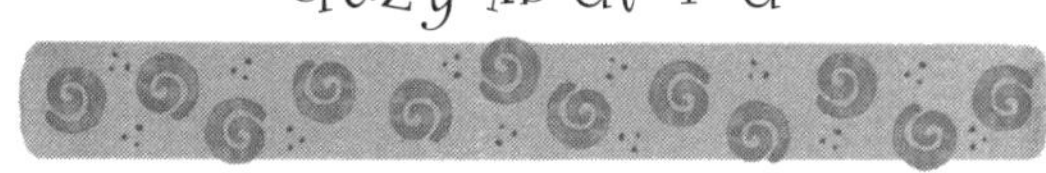

·295·

You always pick the perfect greeting card.

·296·

You never blame my over-the-top behavior on PMS.

·297·

You taught me how to play strip poker. Wow, what a night *that* was.

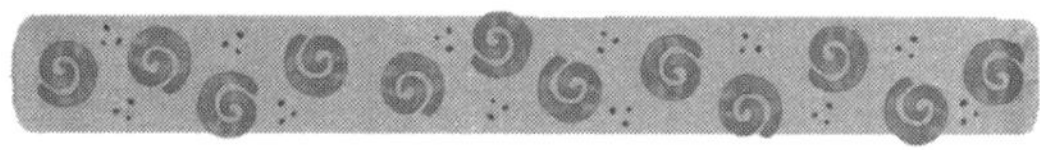

·298·

Before you left on your last business trip, you

a. promised to phone me every night

b. offered me your pajamas to sleep in

c. gave me a bottle of your cologne

d. told me you'd miss me every moment

e. all of the above

·299·

I'm absolutely certain that ours is the most romantic love story in history.

·300·

What you want to do on Saturday night is what I want to do, too. Even if you want to clean the garage.

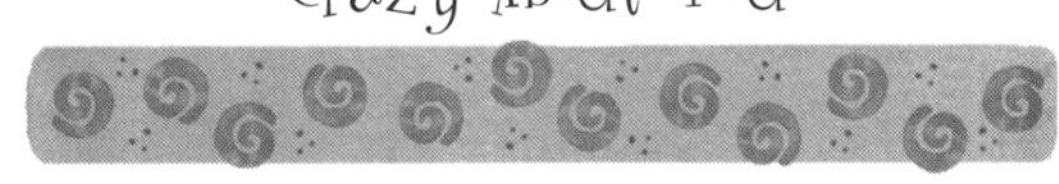

·301·

You don't go berserk if I kiss you in public, but I *will* try to control myself.

·302·

You have perfect pitch and a gorgeous singing voice, and you let me sing along even though I can't carry a tune.

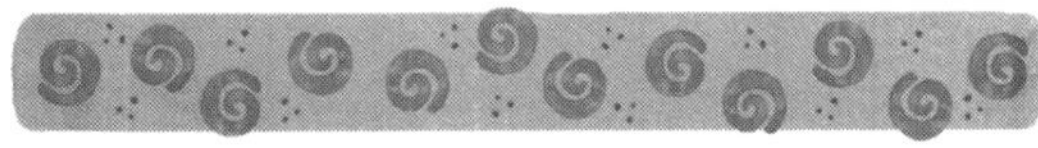

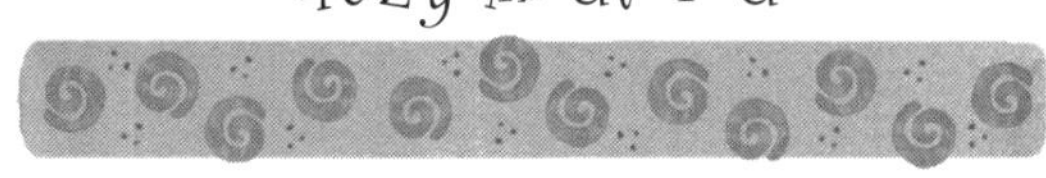

·303·

When I tell you a story, I try not to go off on tangents because I know it drives you crazy. And when you tell me one, you add a few extra paragraphs because you know I revel in the juicy details.

·304·

I forgive you for forgetting my existence during Sunday afternoon football games on TV. Enjoy yourself.

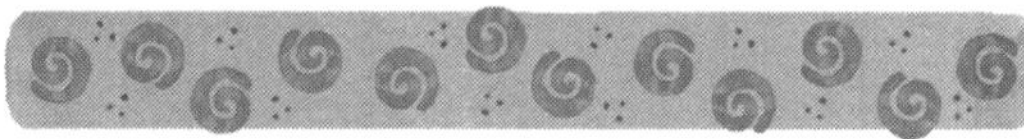

·305·

Okay, I admit it: I'm in seventh heaven when you occasionally treat me like a little girl—as long as you remember that most of the time I'm a grown-up woman.

·306·

When you don't call, I stand over the phone and ask it to ring.

·307·

You keep popping up
in my dreams.

·308·

I wrote a poem about you.

·309·

I do nice things for you without
even telling you—but you
always guess who did them.

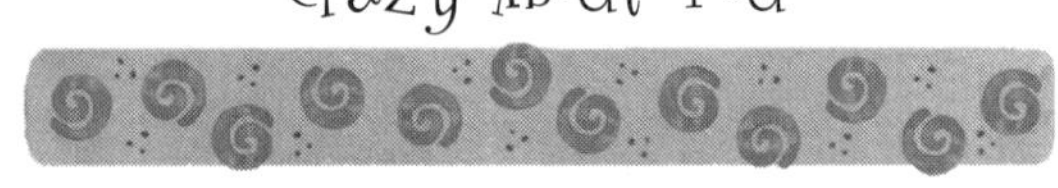

· 310 ·

You don't expect me to like the Three Stooges. Or the Marx Brothers. Or W. C. Fields. And you don't accuse me of having no sense of humor because I can't stand them.

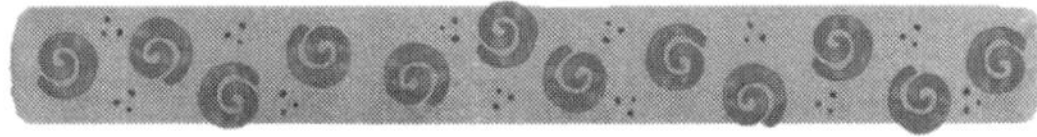

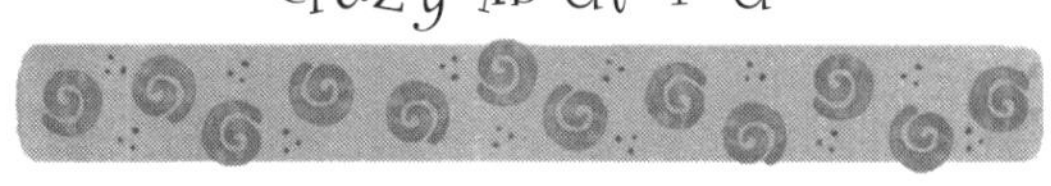

Diapers don't scare you—even used ones. If it's your turn to feed the baby in the middle of the night, you get up without grumbling. You take your turn at the pediatrician. What a great father you are.

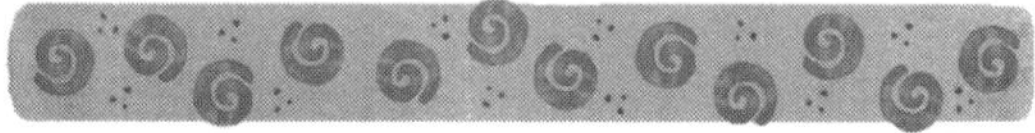

You don't leave your

a. dirty dishes

b. dirty clothes

c. dirty towels

d. all of the above

lying around for me to deal with.

When we drove through wine country, you restrained yourself admirably so I could taste vino to my heart's content and you could stay sober behind the wheel.

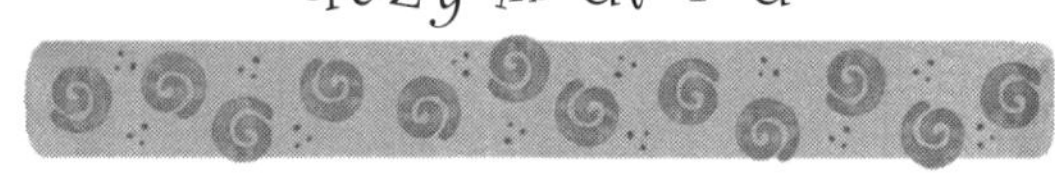

·314·

You remember the most important moments of our romance as well as I do.

·315·

We agree on how to handle our finances.

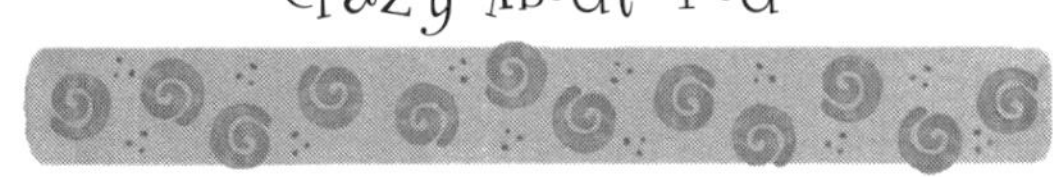

·316·

We don't try to run each other's lives.

·317·

You tore right out to the drugstore to fill my prescription when I was too sick to do it myself.

·318·

You're not embarrassed to let me see you cry.

·319·

I can tolerate the thought of getting stuck in an elevator—but only if it's with you.

·320·

You kept your arm around me all the way through my grandfather's funeral, to comfort me.

·321·

You jolly me out of my bad moods. Well, you *try* to jolly me out of my bad moods.

·322·

You're never suspicious of me—because you know you don't have to be.

·323·

Footsie is your favorite game.

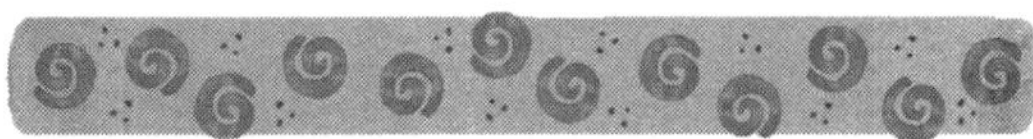

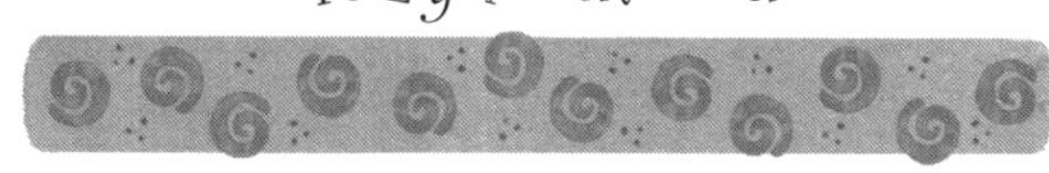

·324·

Mother's Day wouldn't be Mother's Day for me without you. Literally.

·325·

If you wanted me to, I'd hold your hand at the dentist.

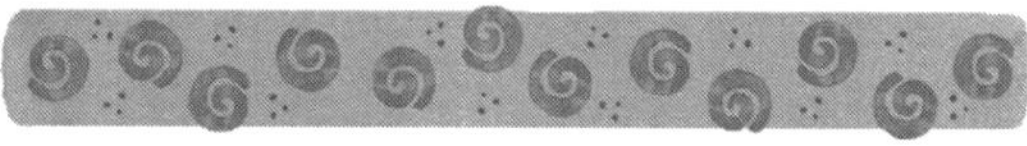

·326·

If you wanted me to,
I'd be your date at your
high school reunion.

·327·

If you wanted me to,
I'd go with you
to visit your least
favorite relatives.

·328·

Except for the fact that it means you're leaving for a few days, I get a tremendous kick out of packing your suitcase for you. (Hey, don't forget to check between the socks—I left you a little present there.)

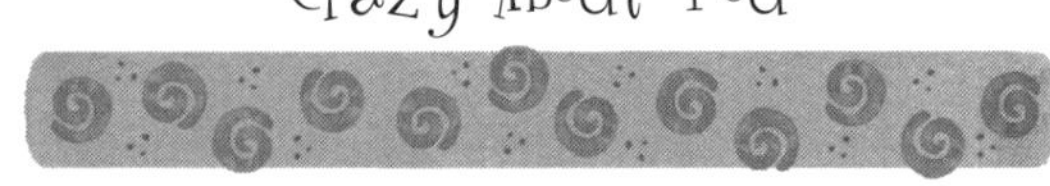

·329·

You threw a party for my birthday, and you did it all yourself.

·330·

It's bliss to spend quiet time in the hot tub with you.

·331·

You can tease me (gently) out of my sillier behavior.

·332·

You don't shriek and run when I discuss pelvics, mammograms, yeast infections, and other yucky female stuff.

·333·

In a room full of hundreds of people, I'd still pick you out for my one-and-only.

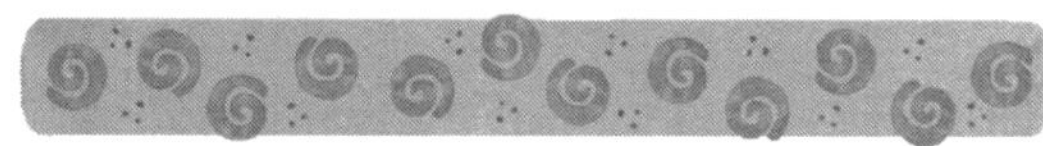

·334·

When I came home from work on Friday night, you had a bottle of wine cooling, soft music on the stereo, and a dozen candles lit for romance.

·335·

You'd never refer to me as

a. the little woman

b. my ball and chain

c. my old lady

(Not if you wanted to live

to see another day.)

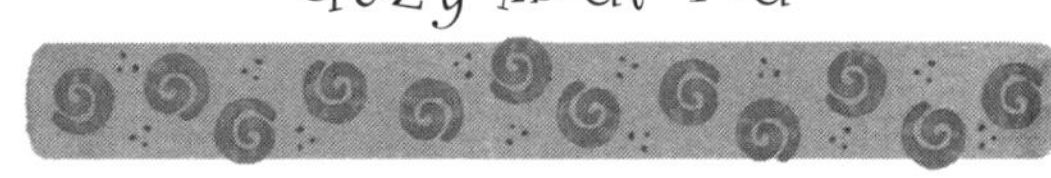

·336·

You don't make me ask you fifteen times to take out the garbage or load the dishwasher or pick up the dry cleaning. Three times usually does the trick.

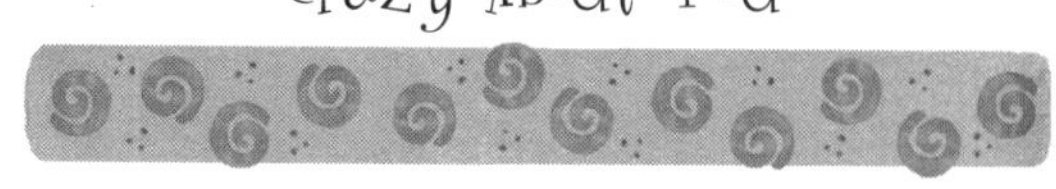

·337·

The bartender brought me a drink sent by an anonymous admirer—and it turned out to be you.

·338·

You don't mind if I wear my tatty old shorts and ripped T-shirts around on a Saturday morning, but you're pleased as punch when I change to my sexiest black dress to go out on Saturday night.

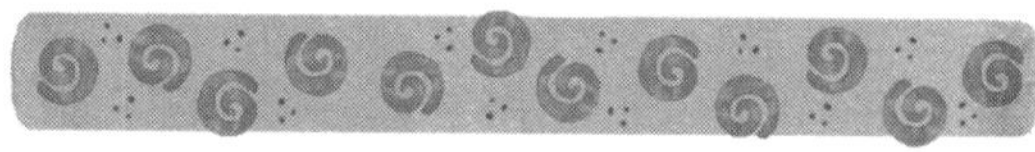

·339·

If I'm not around to hear someone say something nice about me, you pass along the compliment.

·340·

When I met you I bought new sheets for my bed. Then I bought a new bed.

·341·

You gave me a bottle of real perfume—not cologne, but the real thing.

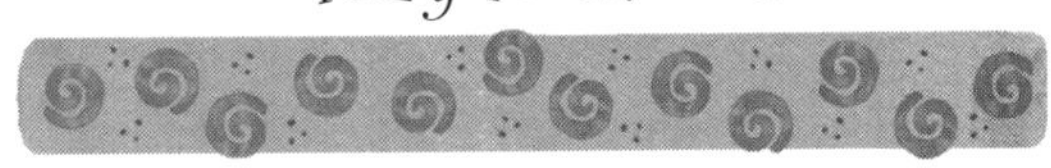

·342·

I'm actually learning to cook.

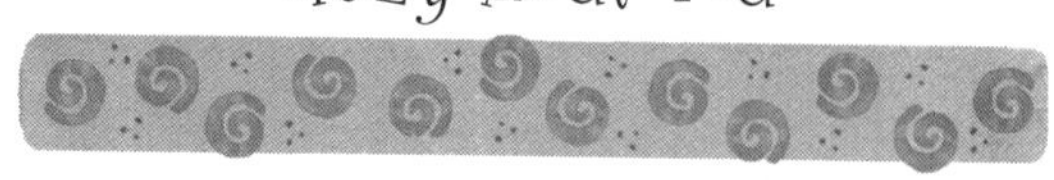

You don't expect me to ask your permission to do whatever I want to do, but you definitely want to be consulted when my activities have an impact on you. That's reasonable, and I go for reasonable.

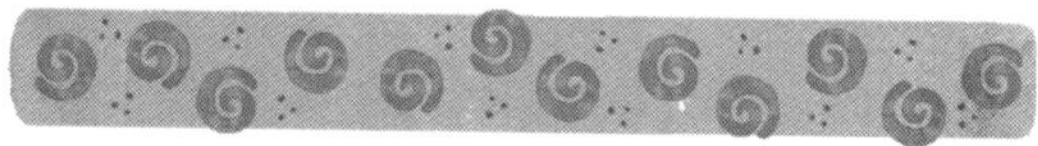

·344·

I will never lie to you.
I may fudge a little,
but I won't lie.

·345·

You don't always ask for my advice, but when you do it's because you really want it.

·346·

You're as interested in the shenanigans of my family as you are in the shenanigans of your family.

·347·

You took sexy pictures of me—but I know you'll never, ever show them to anyone else. (If you do, I'll hire a hit man to push a button on you.)

·348·

When I get into one of those monomaniacal moods in which I have to
a. clean the entire house from top to bottom
b. weed, prune, mulch, feed, and water the whole garden
c. rearrange all the furniture
d. file or dispose of every piece of paper in my office
e. go through all the closets and throw out every item of unnecessary clothing
f. remake myself from hair to toenails
you don't try to stop me.

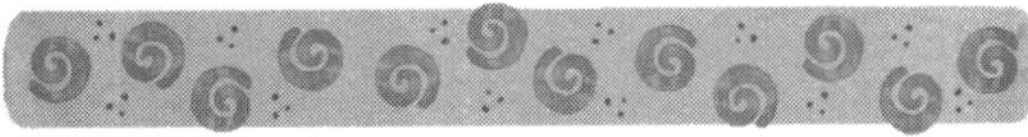

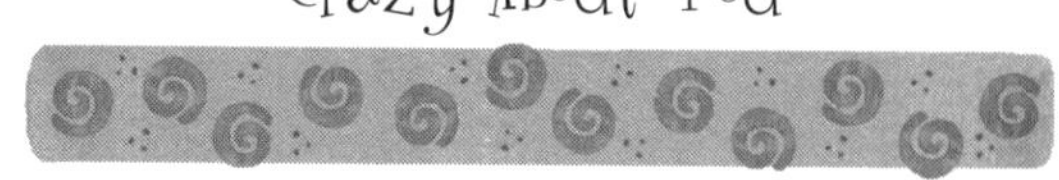

·349·

We have private jokes, signals, and songs.

·350·

I call you from the airport, just to chat for a few more minutes.

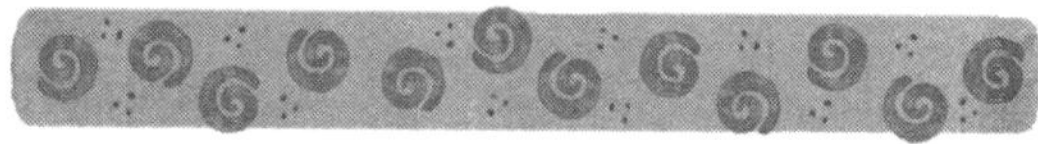

·351·

You took me to the bridal suite of my favorite hotel, even though it's been *aeons* since I was a bride.

·352·

When you were downsized, you licked your wounds, made a plan, and went after what you wanted—and I'll always be there to cheer you on, no matter how long the dry season lasts.

·353·

You don't take me too seriously when I'm acting like a control freak. Hang in there, I'm working on it.

·354·

You'd never open my mail. Not that there's *anything* I wouldn't want you to see.

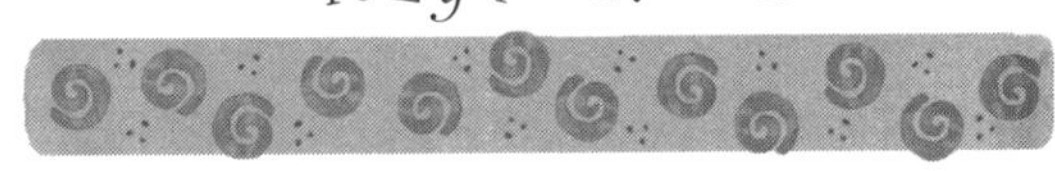

·355·

You took me to my first karaoke club and now I'm addicted and it's all your fault.

·356·

You loved me before, during, and after menopause.

·357·

We don't play mind games
on each other.

·358·

If we don't go home together,
you call to make sure
I got there safely.

·359·

When *you* have the flu, you don't turn into a whiny two-year-old.

·360·

When *I* have the flu,
you act like Florence
Nightingale, bless your heart.

·361·

When *we* have the flu,
we crawl out of bed
together to make soup.
In sickness and in health . . .

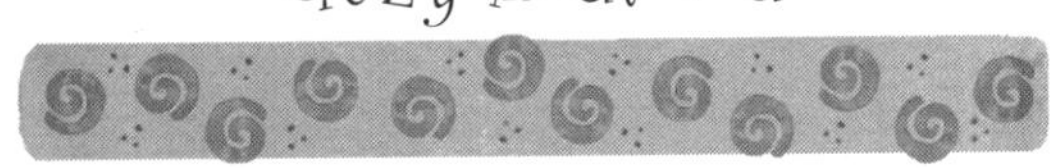

·362·

You root for me when I'm trying to lose those extra pounds, but you tell me you appreciate me just the way I am.

·363·

You drove me to work all week while my car was being repaired.

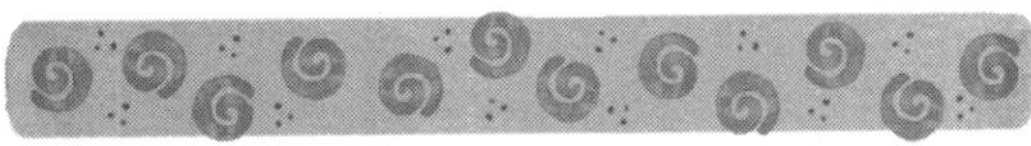

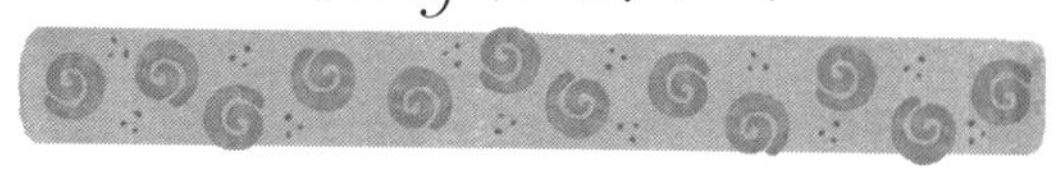

·364·

I understand perfectly that you have to have nights out with the boys, and you understand that I need my nights out with the girls, too.

·365·

Good manners are as important to you as they are to me.

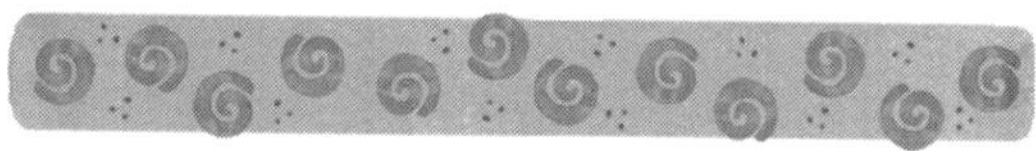

·366·

You notice when something is bothering me and you ask me about it. Most guys would pretend nothing was wrong until whatever it was either went away or turned into a crisis.

·367·

I love to get dressed in front of you because you love to watch.

·368·

I've introduced you
to *all* my friends.

·369·

The tomatoes from your garden
are the best I've ever tasted.

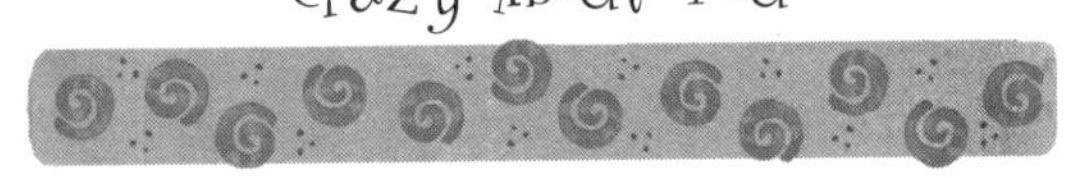

·370·

You were *very* impressed with my résumé. And I was *very* impressed with yours.

·371·

I call you first when there's

a. good news

b. bad news

c. no news, but I just feel like talking

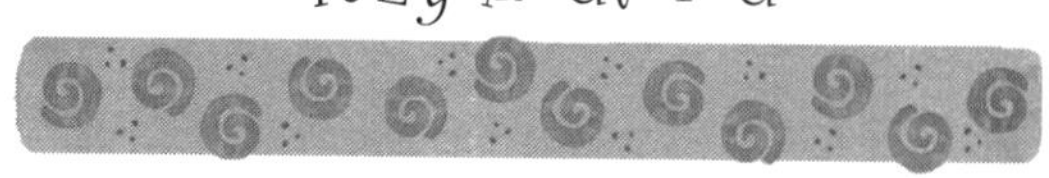

·372·

You clip interesting newspaper items for me.

·373·

Helping you clean out the basement is a lark.

·374·

I know all your favorites—sandwich, movie star, rock group, cartoon, author, car, city, soda, vegetable, and holiday.

·375·

When I told you I'm lonely on the nights you're away, you bought me the cutest puppy in the world to keep me company.

·376·

You ran my successful campaign for school board.

·377·

You keep my photo in your wallet.

·378·

You bought me my first diamond.

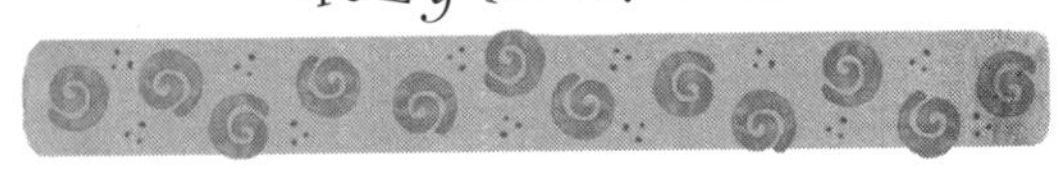

·379·

I love the kids, but I look forward to an empty nest and having you all to myself again.

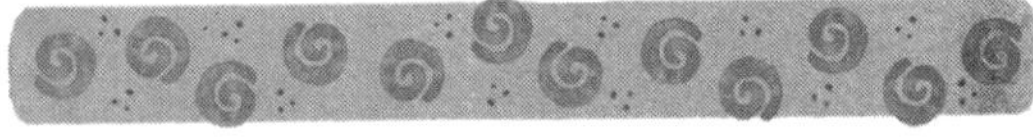

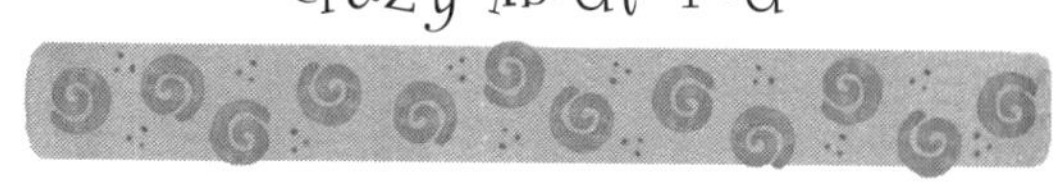

·380·

I love the kids, but I treasure the nights *we* have together when *they* stay over at their grandparents'.

·381·

I love the kids, but I'm glad we have a sturdy lock on our bedroom door.

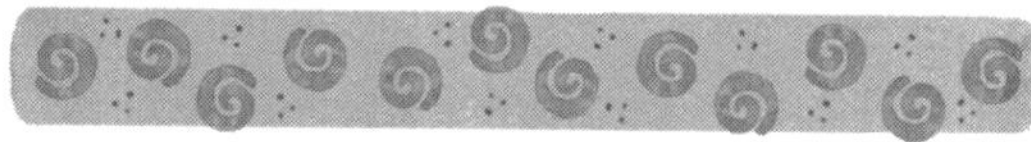

When I'm angry at you,
I try to remember how
much I worship you when
I'm *not* angry at you.

·383·

If you're going to be late,
you always call so I won't worry.
And I do the same for you.

·384·

You surprised me
with a celebration to
renew our wedding vows.

·385·

You received an inheritance
and you offered to
share it with me.

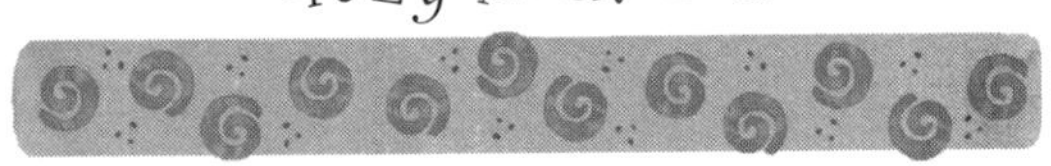

·386·

I feel better,
magically, when
you're near me.

·387·

You're number one
on my speed dial.

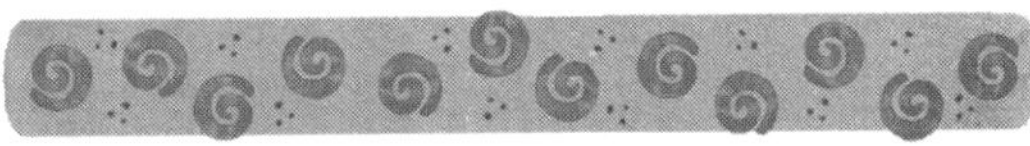

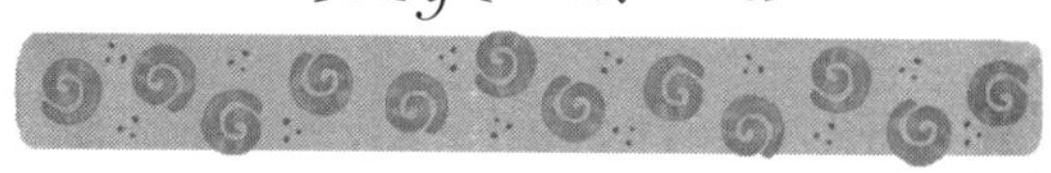

·388·

When I have a problem at work, you listen attentively and ask good questions until I find my way to a solution by myself.

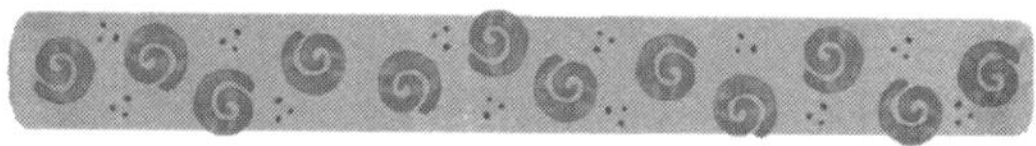

You had the patience
to teach me to play
a. pool
b. bridge
c. chess
d. the guitar
e. all of the above

·390·

I'm flattered when you dress up nicely to take me out on a date.

·391·

We stole an afternoon and spent it in bed. And you didn't once mention the work you should have been doing.

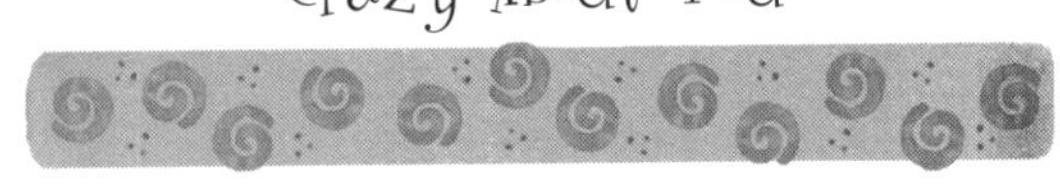

·392·

Buying presents for you is a joy.

·393·

You'd never hold my
past against me.

·394·

When we're on vacation, you don't expect me to be your travel agent, your tour guide, or your translator.

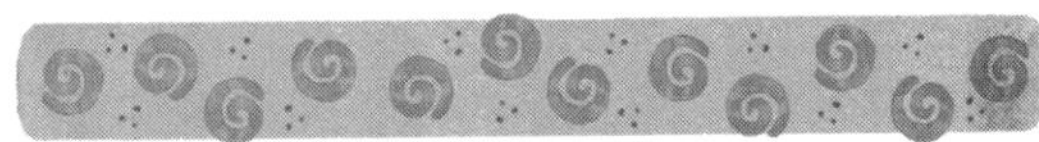

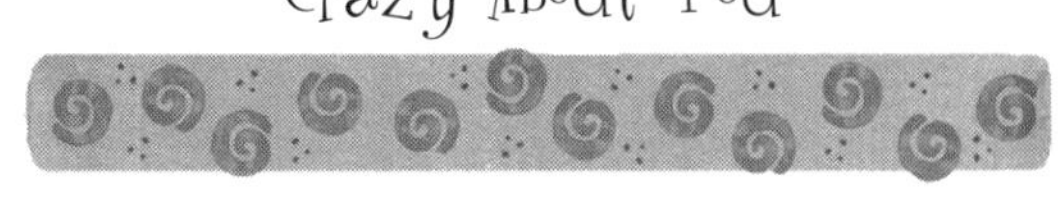

·395·

You're never too tired
to build a cozy fire
in the fireplace.

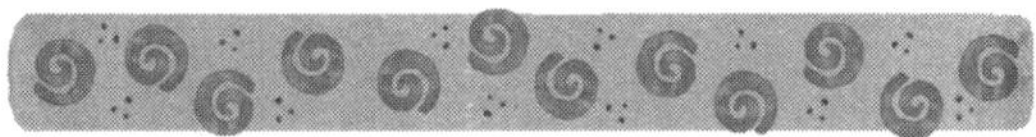

·396·

You always believe the best of me.

·397·

I just can't keep my hands off you.

·398·

I won't mind a bit if you turn on a light and read in bed when I'm trying to fall asleep.

·399·

When you're driving me nuts, I've learned to walk away for a five-minute time-out and come back ready to be sane. Until the next episode.

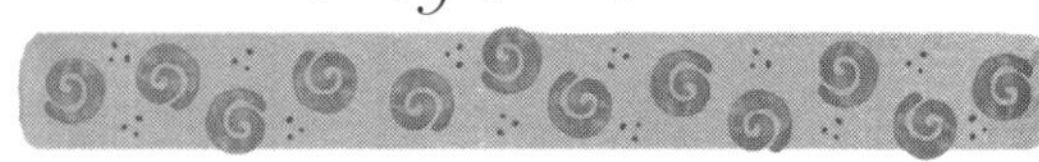

·400·

Call me anytime your computer has a glitch. I'll try to fix it.

·401·

Wake me anytime you can't sleep. I'll sing you a lullaby until you drift off to dreamland.

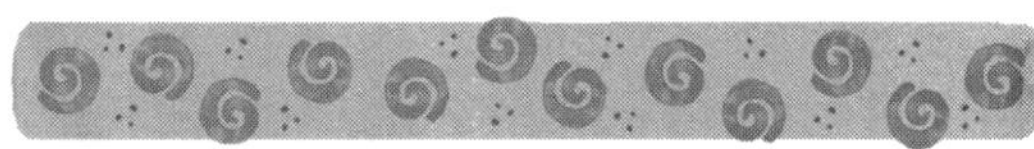

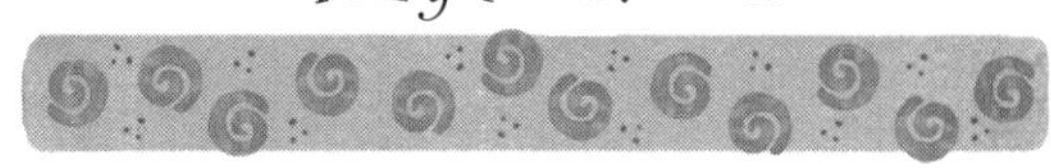

·402·

Let me know anytime your car won't start. I'll race right over to give you a jump.

·403·

You take responsibility for your own life.

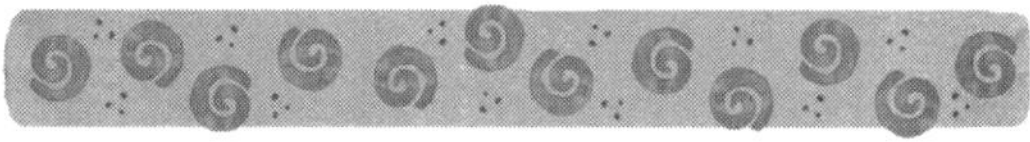

·404·

I admire the way you speak up when

a. injustice is being done

b. there's a misunderstanding

c. someone is spreading false information

d. you have a good idea

e. all of the above

·405·

Being emotional doesn't scare you one bit.

·406·

You're not threatened by my competence.

·407·

You shower me with compliments.

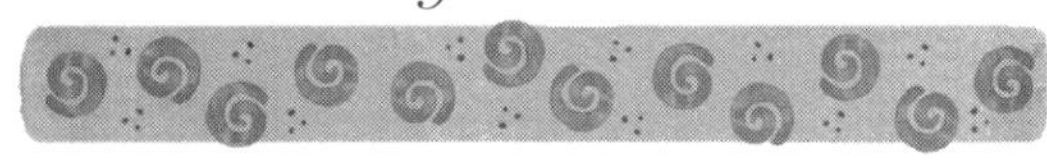

·408·

If my best friend calls ten times a day, you never complain. (If your best friend calls ten times a day, I don't complain either—I turn on the answering machine and get out of the house.)

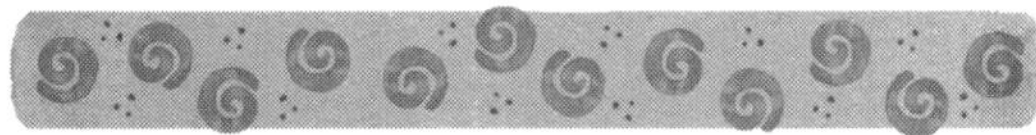

·409·

During the big snowstorm we hunkered down together and never missed the electricity.

·410·

Be prepared is your motto.

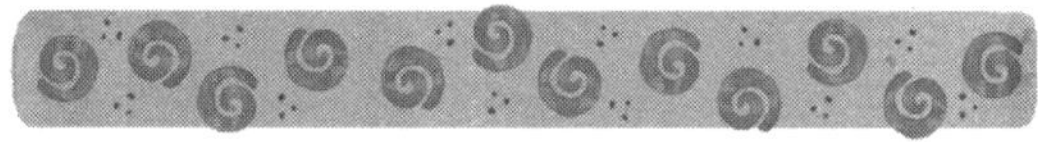

·411·

I was bidding against someone on eBay, and I didn't get what I wanted. It broke my heart—until I found out that *you* were the other bidder.

·412·

I make sure you take your vitamins.

·413·

When I talk, you listen.
When you talk, I listen.

·414·

The first time was pretty good, but the second, third, fourth, fifth . . . it gets better and better.

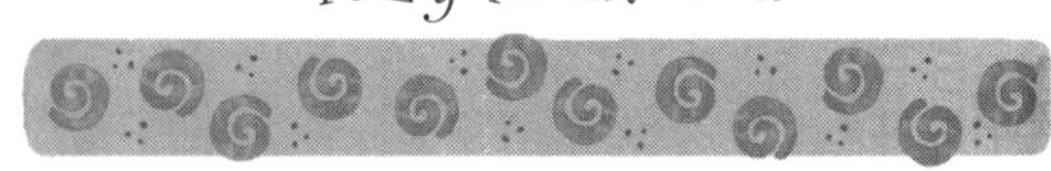

·415·

You catch my spelling and grammar mistakes when I'm writing a business letter.

·416·

You know what size I wear. (What you *don't* know yet is that I don't always wear the same size . . .)

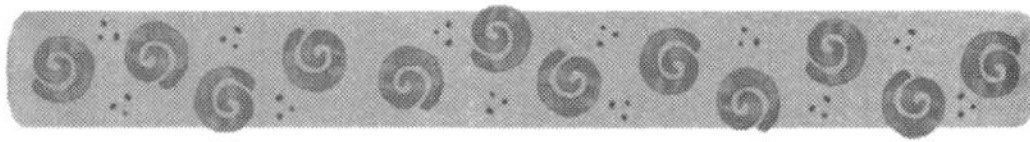

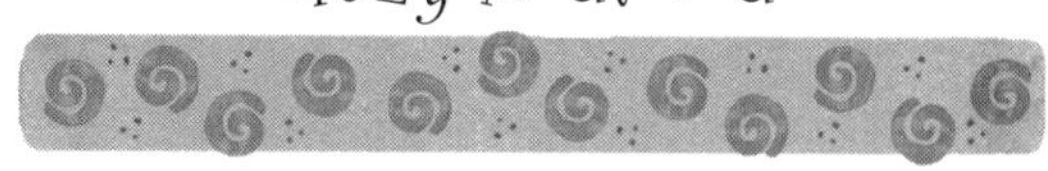

Wedding bells are
ringing in my head.

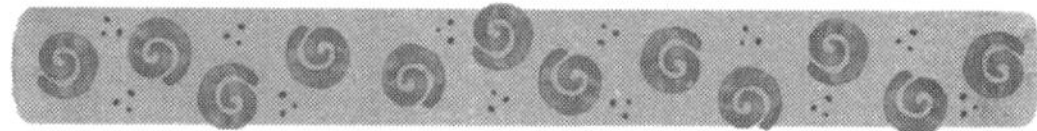

·418·

You got me my own phone line and told the kids they weren't allowed to use it—ever.

·419·

When I ask you to drive slower, you ease up on the accelerator right away.

·420·

I'd skip a rerun of

a. *Star Trek*

b. *Law and Order*

c. *Sex and the City*

d. *Ally McBeal*

e. *Friends*

if you wanted to go out with me that night.

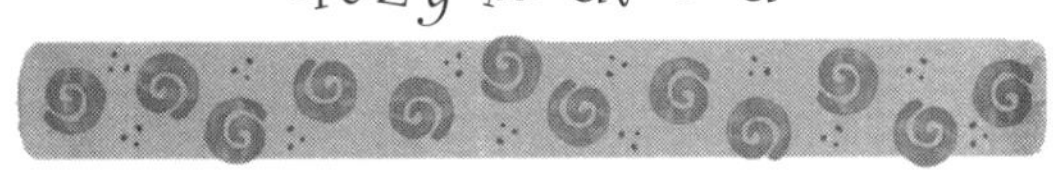

·421·

Valentine's Day is my favorite holiday.

·422·

You don't treat me like your mother, your daughter, your secretary, or your housekeeper.

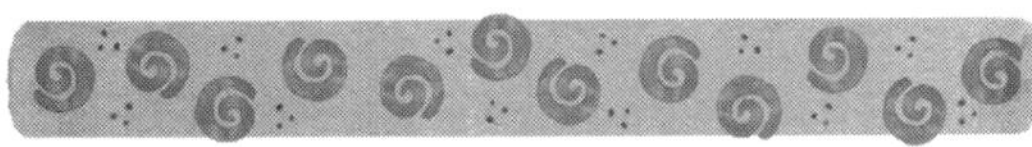

You're not a finicky eater—
but you don't mind that I am.

·424·

I search for you on the Internet.

·425·

Even though you may not understand my decision-making process, you respect my decisions.

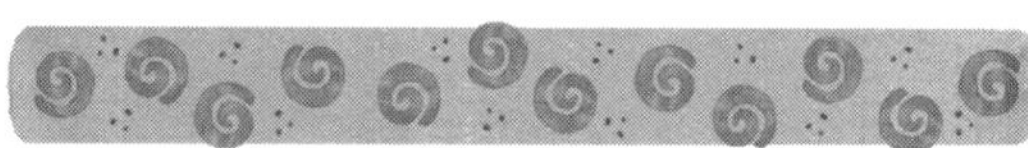

·426·

You always check with me before accepting an invitation that includes both of us.

·427·

You shave before we make love.

·428·

I keep my fridge stocked with a couple of bottles of champagne for our unexpected special occasions. Any excuse will do.

·429·

We never let the sun set on our fights. Even if we can't get to "yes" before midnight, we restore the peace and go to bed friends.

·430·

When you found that memo pad where I wrote your name a dozen times with "Mrs." before it, you said, "Let's set the date."

·431·

You won't let anyone bad-mouth your mother.

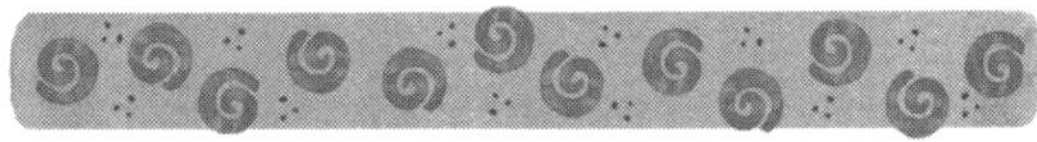

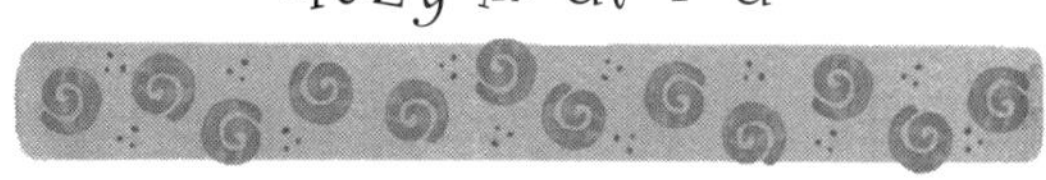

·432·

You'd never try to rearrange

a. my kitchen drawers

b. my desk

c. my living room

d. my calendar

e. my life

unless I asked you to.

·433·

It feels like
Christmas every day.

·434·

I don't mind if your high-school friends come over for an afternoon of beer and sports, but there are limits—and you know what they are.

·435·

You gave me a pair of black leather pants for my birthday.

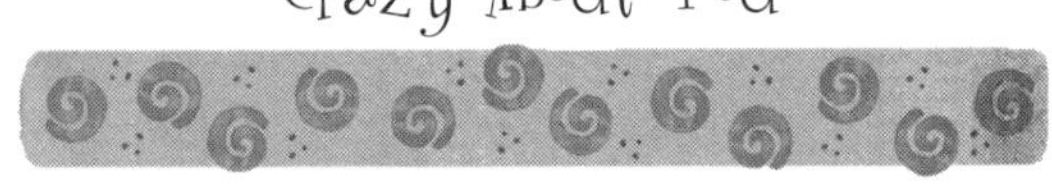

·436·

I treasure the engagement and wedding rings you gave me as symbols of your love and devotion.

·437·

You took a one-day course in massage. Now I'm your slave.

·438·

With you, even moving house is fun. Amazing.

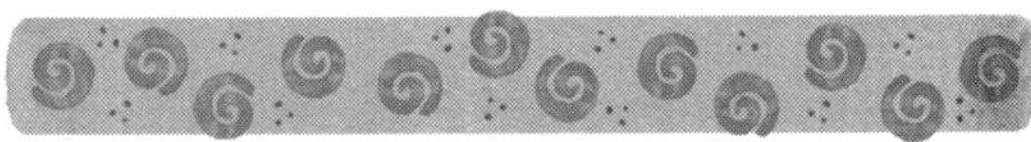

·439·

I have a few guy friends and you're not jealous . . . are you?

·440·

We snuck out and borrowed the kids' sleds to whiz down the snow-packed hill at midnight.

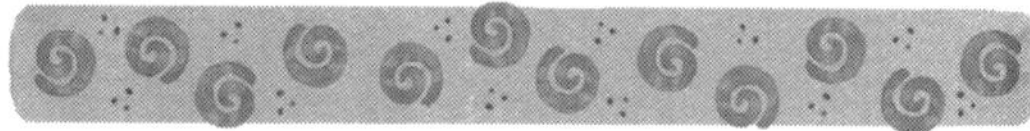

·441·

You gave me your favorite baseball cap.

·442·

We go to as many romantic movies (my choice) as action-adventure movies (yours).

·443·

You polished the silver. I still can't believe it.

·444·

You bought me a slew of audiobooks so I wouldn't be bored on the drive to and from work.

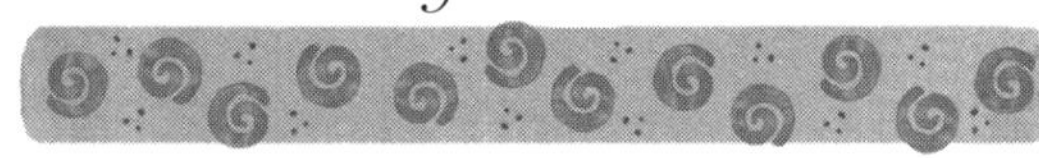

·445·

I'm looking forward to your birthday more than *you* are. Wait till you see what I'm going to do for you.

·446·

We've discussed our relationship a trillion times, but you have patience for discussing it again.

·447·

You're great at long-term planning—but you're even more terrific at spur-of-the-moment fun.

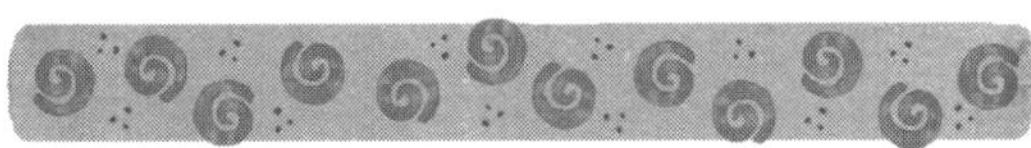

·448·

You have a good heart.

·449·

You're living in the present,
not clinging to the past.

·450·

I have to pinch myself
to believe this is real.

·451·

If I'm in charge of the

a. PTA meeting

b. co-op board

c. church bazaar

d. fund-raiser

e. ad campaign

you follow my plan without arguing or complaining or letting me know you could do it better.

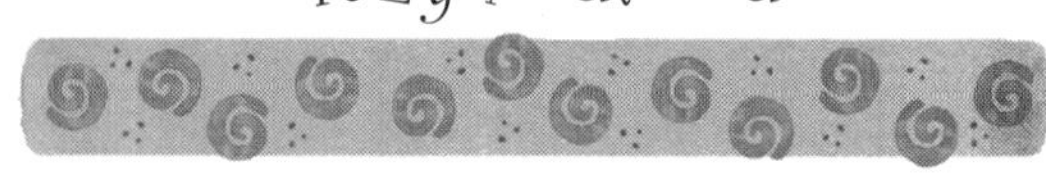

·452·

We were barely acquainted with each other, but you popped open your umbrella and walked me home in the rain.

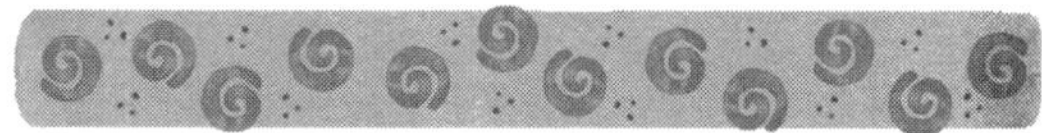

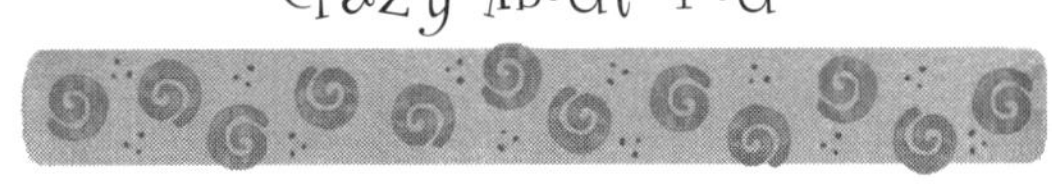

·453·

I remembered to set the alarm for you when you had an early flight to catch.

·454·

It's not beyond your comprehension that there are occasional mornings, afternoons, or nights when I just don't want to make love.

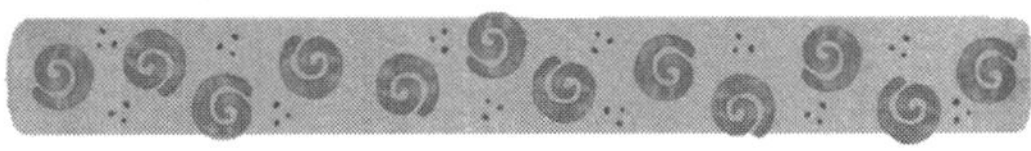

·455·

We laugh at the same jokes.

·456·

You clean the hairs out
of the drain after you shower.

·457·

I try hard not to lose
my temper at you when
you don't deserve it.

·458·

I chose the name of my favorite singer for my bank card PIN, but it was already taken—by you.

·459·

You held the ice pack on my sprained ankle until your hands froze.

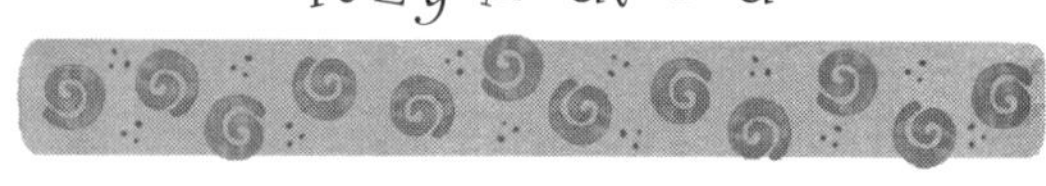

·460·

We can't wait to put our special Christmas ornaments on the tree, because we found them together and each one has a story behind it.

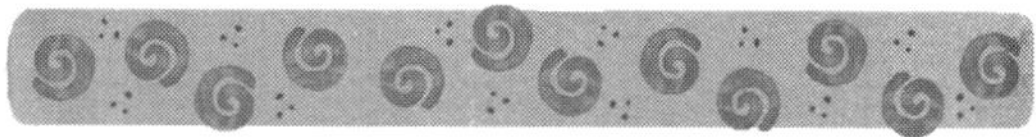

·461·

You've swept me completely off my feet.

·462·

You bought me an antique gold locket and you put your picture in it.

·463·

If anyone says anything nasty about you, I'll take him apart.

·464·

You helped me get through my

a. thirtieth

b. fortieth

c. fiftieth

d. sixtieth

e. seventieth

birthday.

·465·

We argue about politics,
but you never try to make me vote
exactly the way you vote.

·466·

No matter how foolishly
you behave or how wrong
you are, I'll always think
the world of you.

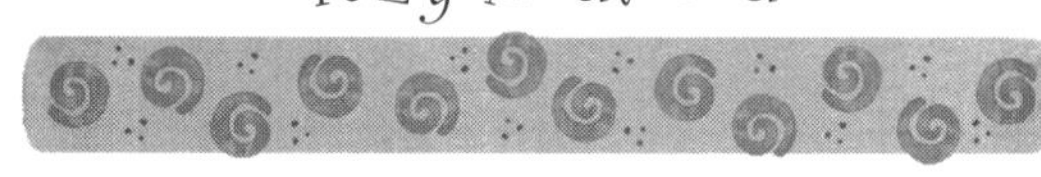

·467·

Scaring me is not something you find amusing, so you've stopped taking insane risks because you know it terrifies me. Thank you, thank you, for giving up bungee jumping, stock-car racing, skydiving, and climbing the Himalayas.

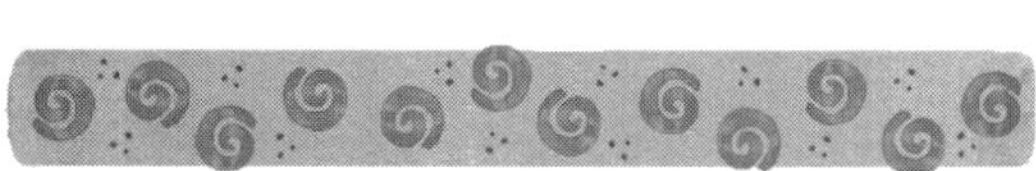

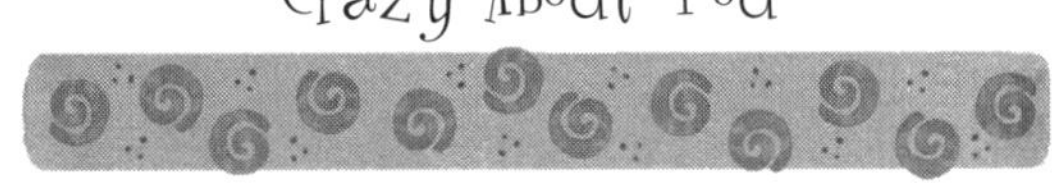

·468·

You're my personal best.

·469·

I want to take you to
the Tunnel of Love.

·470·

Your license plate
spells out my name.

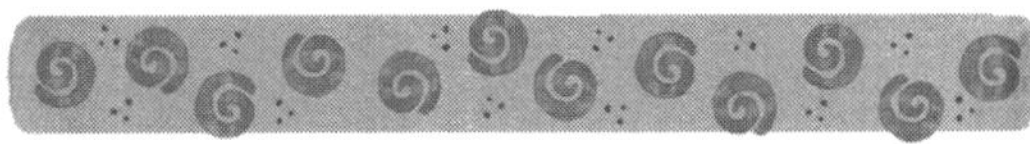

·471·

You figured out all by yourself that if you like seeing me in pretty lingerie, I like seeing you in handsome equivalents.

·472·

I couldn't resist decorating your birthday cake with hearts and flowers.

·473·

I promise I won't raise any of my usual feminist objections if you

a. hold the door

b. hold my chair

c. carry my packages

d. pick up the check

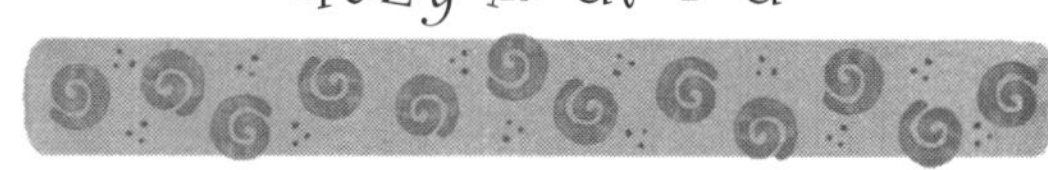

·474·

I made a special trip to the library to borrow that new novel you were panting to read.

·475·

You're not scared of people who are different from you—whatever their age, race, sexual orientation, or ethnicity.

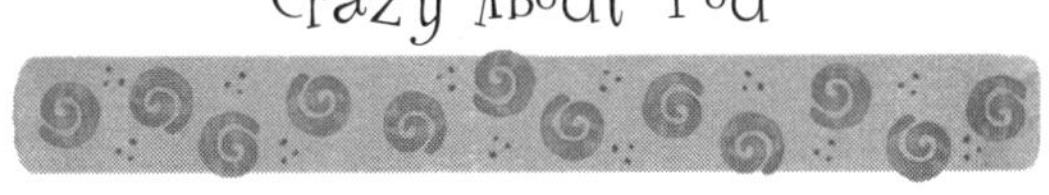

·476·

The word *hypocrisy* isn't even in your vocabulary.

·477·

You try not to fall asleep right after making love. Okay, so you don't always manage it, but I do appreciate your trying.

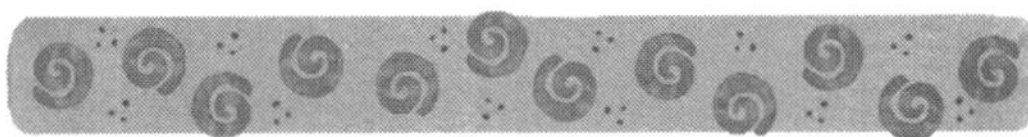

·478·

When we have an argument, I'm around the bend until we make up again.

·479·

You like my girlfriends. (But not *too* much.)

There were mountains of dishes to wash and oceans of straightening up to do after my first big party, so you stayed until four in the morning to give me a hand.

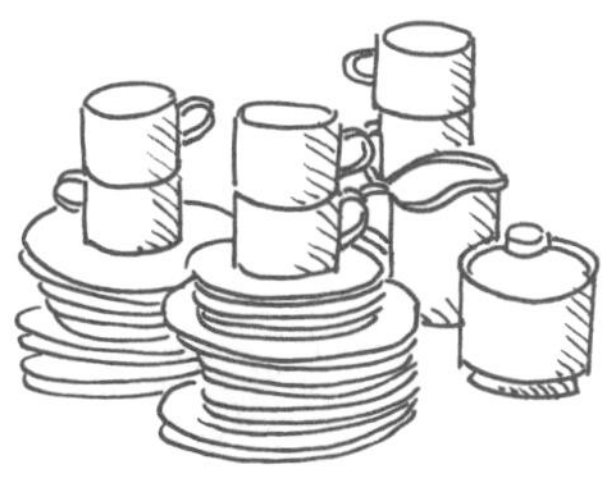

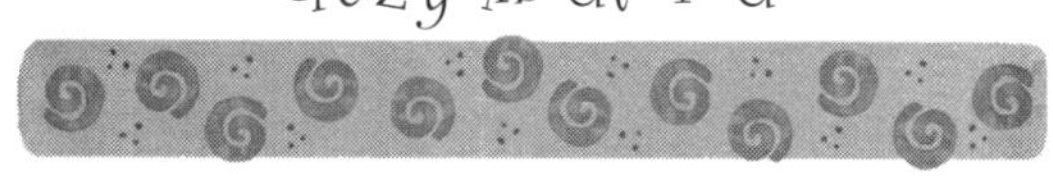

I solemnly swear
I will learn to dote on
a. your mother
b. your sister
c. your closest friend and his wife
but do *not* ask me to open
my heart to your nerdy
sidekick from junior high.

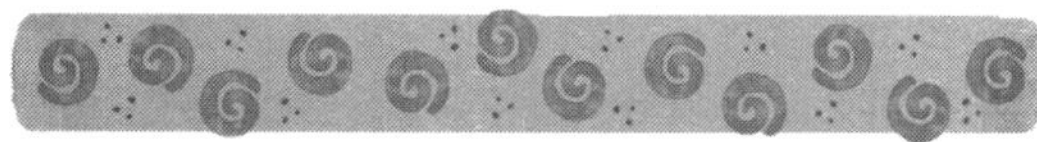

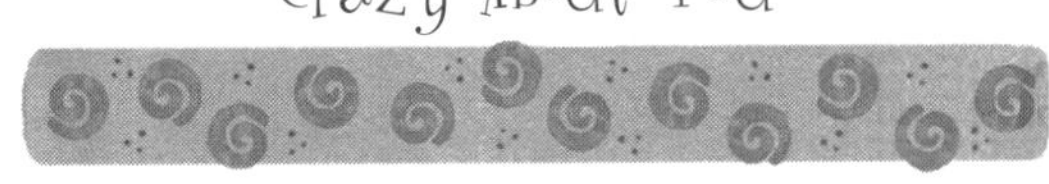

·482·

You get angry on my behalf,
but you let me fight my
own battles—unless
I ask for your help.

·483·

Instead of being a chore,
wrapping all those Christmas
presents was a ball because
you were doing it with me.

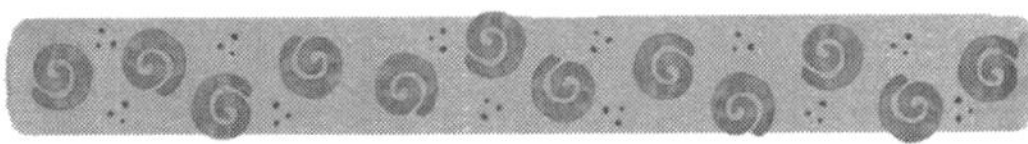

·484·

All right, all right, we can keep your old BarcaLounger even though it makes the den look like a used-furniture showroom.

·485·

I smack my lips over your mom's cooking as much as you do.

·486·

You offered to type my master's thesis. And you praised it to the skies.

·487·

We tell each other our nighttime dreams so we'll know each other better.

·488·

I didn't hesitate to cut in on you when you were dancing with someone else. (After that you danced only with me.)

·489·

My brain, my body, and my instincts all confirm you're the right one for me.

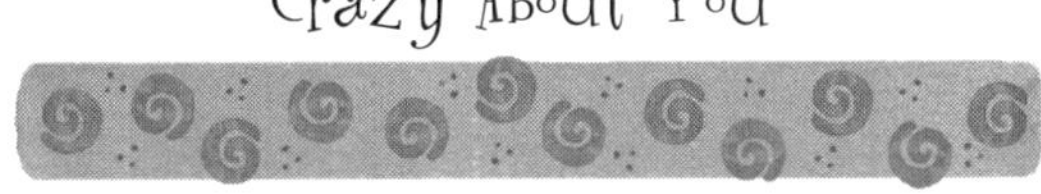

· 490 ·

You've had enough lovers to know how to be a good one yourself, but not so many that I'm jealous.

· 491 ·

I stay awake and keep you company when you're doing the driving at night.

·492·

When you say
you'll call, you do.

·493·

When you say you'll
do something, you will.

·494·

When you say you'll be there, you are.

·495·

You got the kids out of the house when I was trying so hard to study for my final exams.

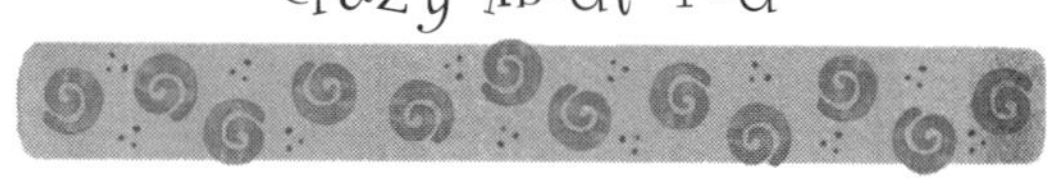

·496·

You don't expect me to read your mind, and I don't expect you to read mine either. A little privacy is a very good thing.

·497·

Occasionally you keep me waiting, but I'd wait for you forever.

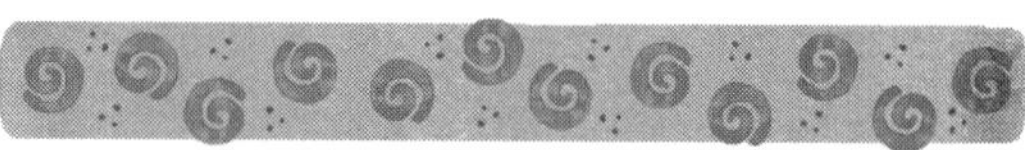

·498·

Ours sounds a lot better to me than *yours* and *mine.*

·499·

I'm grateful to you for biting your tongue when you really feel like saying, "I told you so."

·500·

My grandmother would have approved of you. She was one sharp cookie.

·501·

My father *does* approve of you. He's even sharper than Grandma was.

·502·

You've made me forget all the other men I've ever loved.

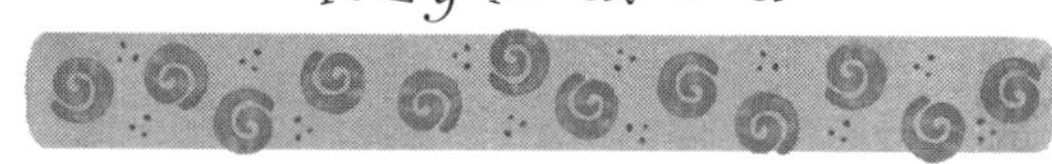

·503·

I'm so involved with you
that it's hard for me to find time
for my dearest friends.

·504·

Smart is as important
to you as *pretty,*
if not more so.

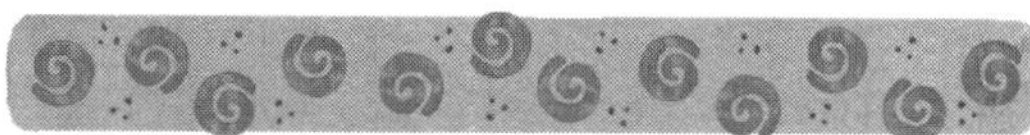

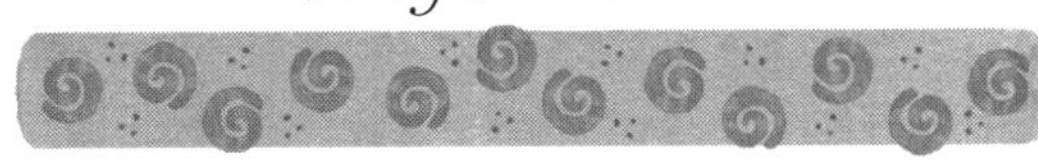

·505·

You bought me the sexiest nightgown I've ever owned. And you insisted I model it for you right away.

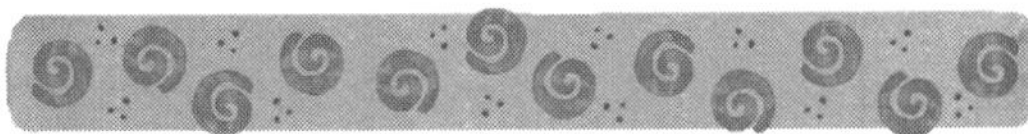

·506·

There are days when I wish we were the only two people in the world.

·507·

I painted my living room your favorite color.

·508·

I'm 100 percent convinced we were made for each other.

·509·

On a life-is-great scale
of one to ten, this moment
with you is a ten.

·510·

I can't wait to be
alone with you.

·511·

I'll always keep your secrets.

·512·

Wherever you are is home to me.

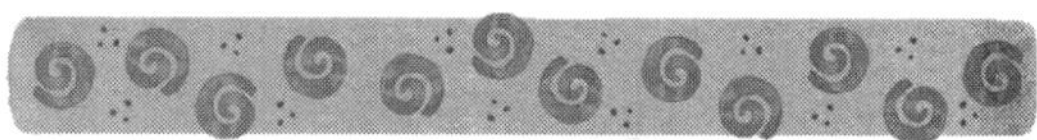